Did you know there is a London,
a Manchester and a Glasgow in Kentucky?
So Elvis could, quite legitimately, have
made a 'London Calling' album...
(Ray Lowry)

"RAT PATROL FROM FORT BRAGG"

BY ALAN PARKER

ABSTRACT SOUNDS PUBLISHING

Rat Patrol From Fort Bragg © Abstract Sounds
Publishing
Text © Alan Parker
Exclusive Distributors: Turnaround Publisher
Services UK
Orders: orders@turnaround.uk.com

First Published in Britain in 2003
by Abstract Sounds Publishing
a division of Abstract Sounds LTD
2 Elgin Avenue London W9 3QP

Reprinted 2004

Email: abstractsounds@btclick.com
Website: www.abstractsounds.co.uk

ISBN 0 95357249 8

Art Direction & design: Kieran MacIver

Cover Idea: David Parker

Editor: Jonathan Richards

Unpublished Photos: Rex Features

(with thanks to Glen Marks)

Clash clothing from the Phil Strongman archive

(photographed by Joe Alvarez)

Printed and bound in the UK

BOOTLEGS

It is illegal to manufacture, distribute or
sell bootleg or counterfeit recordings.
Bootleg CD or vinyl pictured in this
publication is owned by the author, but in no
way was he or Abstract Sounds Publishing
involved in the manufacture, distribution or
sale of these recordings.

Bootlegs are illegal. Pressing and selling
them is illegal.

PHOTOGRAPHIC CREDITS

The author of this work and Abstract Sounds
Publishing have made every effort to credit
all photographs in this publication to their
relevant photographer/owner. All
photographers/owners, where known, have been
contacted for permission to reproduce their
work. Photographers/owners of uncredited work
should contact Abstract Sounds Publishing.

All memorabilia pictured in this book is from
the personal collection of Alan Parker.

www.blackmarketclash.com
(Best Clash web site in the world ever etc...)

(From left to right) Alan Parker, Nick Reynolds
and Mick Jones at The Borderline, summer of 1999.

"ADULTS ARE JUST OBSOLETE CHILDREN... AND TO HELL WITH THEM!"

(DR SEUSS)

Potentially the greatest rock n' roll band in the world ever, The Clash were always more than a mere garage band. Far outliving the punk tag which so many other groups of the same era seemed hopelessly trapped by - not for nothing did Rolling Stone magazine vote 'London Calling' the best album of the Eighties, even if it was recorded and released in 1979! The Clash, in fact, delivered two excellent punk rock albums before unshackling themselves from its limitations and went on to produce three records that would help shape rock n' roll as we now know it. Like all great bands of any era they were - and indeed still are - bootlegged to the hilt. At the time of writing some of the bootlegs are being, for want of a better expression, re-bootlegged! Sony have re-visited their back catalogue surely as much as any record company decently can, yet have so far failed to add any bonus tracks or update any of their original studio albums. Within this publication, I hope to explore what is available out there and just what recorded state it's in.

If anything, being involved in 'Satellite' - the book on the Pistols I did with Paul Burgess - made this book a lot simpler (if I live to be 100, I'll never find the correct words to thank Paul enough, for everything he did on that project, I'm the headstrong bullish one of the pair, you see) because the pit falls now come shrink-wrapped. The whole scene around 'Satellite' made books like this possible on a whole host of bands. Nick Reynolds said to me about three years ago: 'Satellite wasn't so much a book as a template,' and in many ways he was right.
For quite a while after its release, myself and Edward (boss man at Abstract Sounds Publishing) had talked about following it up with one on The Clash. The question then became - who's going to do it? This question was answered by Don Letts in a Times Square diner. He said I should do it myself. It made sense. I've been a Clash fan for years, and given the subject matter I've more to bring to the party than I did for the Pistols.

At this point I'd like to put the cat amongst the pigeons. In the early part of summer (2002) myself and Tony James (Generation X) were taking a cab ride from the apartment building where we both live to Silk Sounds studio in Soho. I asked him if the London SS (incredibly early band featuring Tony, Mick Jones and Brian James) had ever made any recordings, at which point he told me that they hadn't done any recording, but at least half a dozen rehearsals were taped. That I'll give you something to look for next time you're looking bootlegs, because those tapes must exist somewhere... Hopefully this book will shed some light on the depth of the unreleased output by this exceptional British rock band who, unlike so many others, took their message to a world stage.

In case any of you were wondering where the title of this book came from - the answer is quite simple: 'Rat Patrol From Fort Bragg' was the original working title of the album we now call 'Combat Rock', so it seemed only fitting to finally give the title a shelf-life.

I first saw The Clash play live in the early Eighties at King Georges Hall in Blackburn and it's fair to say that they single-handedly changed everything about how I saw the rest of my life from that moment on. By the time you read this book they will be fully paid up members of The Rock n' Roll Hall Of Fame - which in any language is only fair enough. In the words of the group themselves: "This is a public service announcement, with guitars!"

On December 23rd 2002 I was waiting at Heathrow Airport for a flight to Manchester to spend Christmas with my family. Just before our flight was due for boarding, Pete Wylie called me. Joe Strummer was dead. A heart attack at home, he was only 50 years old when he died. By the time I hit my hometown of Blackburn in Lancashire, the normal Christmas staples playing from pub jukeboxes had been swapped for a new 'soundtrack' of The Clash. This would continue for at least five days. My book was almost finished and my hero, one of the men who told me to do this project, was dead.

I had originally intended to dedicate this book to Nils Stevenson, but with the events of December 22nd hanging over it, this one is for Joe...

"We're anti-fascist, anti-violence, anti-racist.

We're against ignorance."

(Joe Strummer)

BRITAIN'S BURNING 'THE LAST BIG EVENT BEFORE WE ALL GO TO JAIL'

THE CLASH

THE SAINTS CHERRY VANILLA

SUBWAY SECT
STINKY TOYS
RICH KIDS
SNATCH
SLITS
SHAG NASTY

4·00 – 10·30
JULY 17 1977

BIRMINGHAM
RAG MARKET

TOM ROBINSON BAND

COMPERE JOHN 'PUNK' PEEL

ALL THIS AND MORE
AT THE RAG MARKET BIRMINGHAM
NEAR NEW CROSS STATION.
TICKETS NOW AVAILABLE FROM:
VIRGIN RECORD SHOPS IN: BIRMINGHAM,
COVENTRY, LIVERPOOL, LEEDS, MAN-
-CHESTER, ALSO RE-CHORDS in DERBY.
MUSIC MACHINE-WORCESTER. MUSIC CRAFT
-TELFORD. TERRY BLOOD-STAFFORD.
GRADUATE RECORDS-DUDLEY. SUNDOWN-
WOLVERHAMPTON. H.M.V-LIECESTER.
THEATRE BOOKINGS-LONDON. BY POST
TO: ENDALE ASSOCIATES, RUTLAND HOUSE,
BIRMINGHAM 3.

Another Endale Assosiates / B. Rhodes Production

THE CLASH OFFICIAL UK DISCOGRAPHY.

"Using pop media to perpetuate radical political views, a cross between The Monkees and The Red Brigade, definitely the new MC5."
(Words to the wise, UK music press)

All releases covered in this section are currently available on CD format at the time of writing (late 2002/early 2003. Notes are also included regarding anything differing from the original UK vinyl releases.

---

(1) THE CLASH

COLUMBIA RECORDS 495344 2
RECORDED † CBS STUDIOS, LONDON

(RUNNING TIME: 35 MINUTES 20 SECONDS)
8TH APRIL 1977.

I'M SO BORED WITH THE USA
WHITE RIOT
HATE & WAR
WHAT'S MY NAME
DENY
LONDON'S BURNING
CAREER OPPORTUNITIES
CHEAT
PROTEX BLUE
POLICE & THIEVES
48 HOURS
GARAGELAND

Line-up for this album was: Mick Jones (guitar/vocal), Joe Strummer (guitar/vocal), Paul Simonon (bass guitar) and Terry Chimes aka Tory Crimes (drums). Often referred to by some fans as 'Clash 1', this self-titled debut album was recorded and mixed, like so many punk debut albums, in a matter of days. Mick Jones has claimed in some interviews that he took so much speed during the recording of this album, he didn't remember making it!

(Author's Notes) In the beginning, we fell in love with The Clash en-masse. They seemed to offer some kind of new hope. Much as I loved The Pistols I'd never been to a Berlin Wall, so it all seemed very removed from our streets. The Clash spoke to you directly whether you lived in London or any other part of the country. These songs made sense instantly to working class street kids. I had to replace their first album 6 months to the day after I had bought it because it had already worn out! At last... the revolution was on.

"Within a year, The Pistols had self-destructed, The Damned disbanded (temporarily, at least), leaving the Clash as the unchallenged standard-bearers of the movement on the strength of a record that reverberated for a full 20 months before the follow-up."
(Dominic Pedler/Record Collector)

"We know the blacks have got their thing sewn up. They got their own culture, but the young white kids don't have nothing."

(Mick Jones)

(2) THE CLASH

EPIC RECORDS   495345 2

(RUNNING TIME: 43 MINUTES 28 SECONDS)
1978.

CLASH CITY ROCKERS*
I'M SO BORED WITH THE USA
REMOTE CONTROL
COMPLETE CONTROL*
WHITE RIOT*
(WHITE MAN) IN HAMMERSMITH PALAIS*
LONDON'S BURNING
I FOUGHT THE LAW*
JANIE JONES
CAREER OPPORTUNITIES
WHAT'S MY NAME
HATE & WAR
POLICE & THIEVES
JAIL GUITAR DOORS*
GARAGELAND

Line-up for this album was: same as above plus Nicky Headon aka Topper Headon (drums) on songs marked *
Basically a re-issue of the original USA version of the debut album, itself issued much later than the UK release and featuring extra tracks to give a bigger picture of where the group were at. This version of the album was also issued on vinyl in Japan at the time under the title 'Pearl Harbour'

"It's a common thing to hear from Clash fans that 'the group changed my life'. And how many bands can claim that?"

(Pat Gilbert/Mojo Magazine)

"I vote for the weirdo, I vote for the loonies, I vote for the people off the left wall, I vote for the individuals."

(Joe Strummer)

(3) GIVE 'EM ENOUGH ROPE

COLUMBIA RECORDS   495346 2
RECORDED # BASING STREET STUDIOS, LONDON
& AUTOMATT, SAN FRANCISCO IN SUMMER 1978.

(RUNNING TIME: 37 MINUTES 2 SECONDS)
10TH NOVEMBER 1978.

ENGLISH CIVIL WAR
TOMMY GUN
JULIE'S BEEN WORKING FOR THE DRUG SQUAD
LAST GANG IN TOWN
GUNS ON THE ROOF
DRUG STABBING TIME
STAY FREE
CHEAPSKATES
ALL THE YOUNG PUNKS (NEW BOOTS AND CONTRACTS)

Line-up for this album was: Mick Jones (guitar/vocal), Joe Strummer (guitar/vocal), Paul Simonon (bass guitar) and Topper Headon (drums).
Original UK vinyl copies came with a now very collectable poster, which is featured in the gatefold of the CD booklet.

(Authors Notes) When this album came out, 'our gang' adopted 'Stay Free' as our theme - even though we'd never met a living soul who had been to prison. Truth was it just seemed like Mick was speaking directly to us, and again, we had never met him. The free poster spent 7 years on walls in various houses and flats before finally falling to pieces, what was left of it ended up in a scrapbook. If push comes to shove this is my favourite Clash album, but to me that is far too hard a choice to make.

"It's not politics - just the difference between right and wrong."

(Paul Simonon)

COLUMBIA RECORDS   495347 2
RECORDED ⏺ WESSEX STUDIOS, LONDON

(RUNNING TIME: 65 MINUTES 7 SECONDS)
14TH DECEMBER 1979.

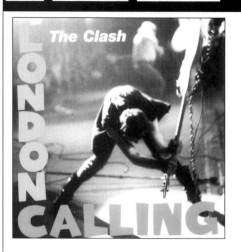

LONDON CALLING
BRAND NEW CADILLAC
JIMMY JAZZ
HATEFUL
RUDIE CAN'T FAIL
SPANISH BOMBS
THE RIGHT PROFILE
LOST IN A SUPERMARKET
CLAMPDOWN
THE GUNS OF BRIXTON
WRONG 'EM BOYO
DEATH OR GLORY
KOKA KOLA
THE CARD CHEAT
LOVER'S ROCK
FOUR HORSEMEN
I'M NOT DOWN
REVOLUTION ROCK
TRAIN IN VAIN

Line-up for this album was: Mick Jones (guitar/vocal), Joe Strummer (guitar/vocal), Paul Simonon (bass/vocal) and Topper Headon (drums/percussion). Original vinyl copies came as two albums in a single sleeve, and sold at the price of a single album. Should have been issued in a sleeve featuring Elvis Presley, but due to major legal problems with both Gracelands and The Elvis Estate the idea was canned. The resulting sleeve echoes Presley's debut in its typography and black and white main image.

(Author's Notes) I was sat in someone's bedroom when this album first appeared in my life. A double? We thought only early Seventies rock bands made double albums, but soon found out we were wrong. I remember singing 'Card Cheat' in my head on the walk home. Then asking my Dad the next day if I could borrow some extra money to buy the album. I used the argument that it was a double and would last for ages, so I wouldn't be borrowing anything else for, well, ages. At school it was the 'soundtrack' in our music room for the best part of a year.

"Some dimwits accused us of being fascist. Really it's saying that white people are so fucked up and intellectual that they can't seem to get any unified thing together."
(Joe Strummer)

"I don't think I'd make such a great rioter..."
(Mick Jones)

White Stripes
New album: The only interview

New! More reviews
The world's best writers! 180 CDs!

MOJO
Music Magazine

MARCH
2003 · £3.50

THE CLASH

THE LIBERTINES
BEDSIT HEDONISM WITH PUNK'S YOUNG ROMANTICS

THE WARLOCKS
MAGIC AND NOISE!

PLUS: FIRST EVER READERS' POLL RESULTS

THE INSIDE STORY OF THE YEAR THEY LOST CONTROL!
JOE REMEMBERED

THE TOP 50 PUNK ALBUMS
PISTOLS TO NIRVANA

THE DAMNED
PUKE, PUNCH-UPS AND PROG!!!

ROGER WATERS
"I'VE NEVER EVEN HEARD THE CLASH!"

No CD? Good... ANARCHY!!! Er, on second thoughts, better have a word with your friendly newsagent.

THE MUSIC MONTHLY

APRIL 84 7

ZIG ZAG

HEROES ★
FOR HIRE
THE CLASH
IN COLOUR

LICOTAGE

GENERAL PUBLIC ★

KILLING JOKE
THE MORAL MINORITY

IT'S THAT MAN AGAIN!
Billy Bragg reviews the singles

JOHN CALE *ZERO*
DEAD OR ALIVE ICONOCL

Joe on the cover of ZigZag April 1984

COLUMBIA RECORDS   495348 2
RECORDED ↑ PLUTO STUDIOS, MANCHESTER.
ELECTRIC LADY, NEW YORK. CHANNEL ONE.
KINGSTON & WESSEX STUDIOS, LONDON

(RUNNING TIME DISC ONE: 70 MINUTES)
(RUNNING TIME DISC TWO: 73 MINUTES)
12TH DECEMBER 1980.

(DISC ONE)

THE MAGNIFICENT SEVEN
HITSVILLE UK
JUNCO PARTNER
IVAN MEETS GI JOE
THE LEADER
SOMETHING ABOUT ENGLAND
REBEL WALTZ
LOOK HERE
THE CROOKED BEAT
SOMEBODY GOT MURDERED
ONE MORE TIME
ONE MORE DUB
LIGHTNING STRIKES (NOT ONCE BUT TWICE)
UP IN HEAVEN (NOT ONLY HERE)
CORNER SOUL
LET'S GO CRAZY
IF MUSIC COULD TALK
THE SOUND OF SINNERS

(DISC TWO)

POLICE ON MY BACK
MIDNIGHT LOG
THE EQUALISER
THE CALL UP
WASHINGTON BULLETS
BROADWAY
LOSE THIS SKIN
CHARLIE DON'T SURF
MENSFORTH HILL
JUNKIE SLIP
KINGSTON ADVICE
THE STREET PARADE
VERSION CITY
LIVING IN FAME
SILICONE ON SAPPHIRE
VERSION PARDNER
CAREER OPPORTUNITIES
SHEPHERDS DELIGHT

Line-up for this album was: Mick Jones (guitar/vocal), Joe Strummer (guitar/vocal), Paul Simonon (bass/vocal), Topper Headon (drums/percussion), Mikey Dread (vocal on Living In Fame), Luke & Ben Gallagher (vocal on Career Opportunities). Guest Musicians: Mickey Gallagher/Timon Dogg/Norman Watt-Roy/JP Nicholson/Ellen Foley/David Payne/Ray Gasconne/Band Sgt Dave Yates/Den Hegarty/Maria Gallagher/Gary & Bill Barnacle/Jody Winscott/Ivan Julien/Noel Tempo Bailey/Anthony Nelson Steele/Lew Lewis/Gerald Baxter-Warman/Terry McQuade/Rudolf Adolphus Jordan and Battersea. The original vinyl copies of this album were a triple album set in a single sleeve that sold for the price of a double (The Clash response to label mate Bruce Springsteen's double 'The River'). It came with a newspaper titled 'The Armagideon Times' Number 3, by cartoonist Steve Bell, now reproduced in a smaller format for the CD version.

(Author's Note) My over-riding memories of this album are two-fold. Firstly, myself and a mate walking from Blackburn to Lower Darwen one very wet Sunday afternoon, just to call on some kid who owned it before we did! And, secondly, Mr Wylde (our English teacher) pointing out that many people would be about to write the word 'Sandinista' all over everything, from school books to the backs of leather jackets, without a clue what the word meant. A lot of people said that an album so big was just too ambitious, but then they said that about 'The White Album'. 'Nuff said.

"I don't know why people are talking about The Clash being a political band. I didn't know who the Prime Minister was until a couple of weeks ago."
(Paul Simonon)

(6) COMBAT ROCK

COLUMBIA RECORDS 495349 2
RECORDED ♦ ELECTRIC LADY, NEW YORK

(RUNNING TIME: 46 MINUTES 25 SECONDS 14TH MAY 1982.

KNOW YOUR RIGHTS
CAR JAMMING
SHOULD I STAY OR SHOULD I GO
ROCK THE CASBAH
RED ANGEL DRAGNET
STRAIGHT TO HELL
OVERPOWERED BY FUNK
ATOM TAN
SEAN FLYNN
GHETTO DEFENDANT
INOCULATED CITY
DEATH IS A STAR

Line-up for this album was: Mick Jones (guitar/vocal), Joe Strummer (guitar/vocal), Paul Simonon (bass/vocal), Topper Headon (drums/percussion), Tymon Dog (piano on Death Is A Star), Poly Mandell (keyboards on Overpowered By Funk), Gary Barnacle (sax on Sean Flynn), Ellen Foley, Allen Ginsberg, Joe Ely and Futura 2000 (various backing vocals). Original vinyl copies came with a fold-out poster of the group (nothing like as rare as the one found in Give 'Em Enough Rope) which is reproduced in a smaller format for the CD version. The working title for this album from day one was 'Rat Patrol From Fort Bragg'.

(Author's Notes) This one took a while to grow on me, but I stuck with it. I remember taping my favourite Clash songs for a lad I worked with at Our Price and he told me not to include anything from 'Combat Rock' on it; rather sneakily, I put the whole album on a 90 minutes tape for him, but I split it up with singles and classic album tracks. A few days later he asked me what all the brilliant unreleased material was on the tape. My face cracked a smile as I told him: 'Combat Rock.'

"Yesterday I thought I was a crud, then I saw the Sex Pistols and I became a King and decided to move into the future. As soon as I saw them I knew that rhythm and blues was dead."
(Joe Strummer)

(7) CUT THE CRAP

COLUMBIA RECORDS 465110 2

(RUNNING TIME: 38 MINUTES 37 SECONDS 4TH NOVEMBER 1985.

DICTATOR
DIRTY PUNK
WE ARE THE CLASH
ARE YOU RED...Y
COOL UNDER HEAT
MOVERS AND SHAKERS
THIS IS ENGLAND
THREE CARD TRICK
PLAY TO WIN
FINGERPOPPIN'
NORTH AND SOUTH
LIFE IS WILD

Line-up for this album was: Joe Strummer (guitar/vocal), Paul Simonon (bass/vocal), Nick Sheppard (guitar/vocal), Vince White (guitar/vocal) and Pete Howard (drums).
The Clash in no more than name alone, an album for completeists only. Might have made an half decent EP. The drummer on this album was almost Steve Grantley, who now plays drums for both Stiff Little Fingers and The Alarm.

CLASH COMMUNIQUE OCTOBER 1985
Wise MEN and street kids together make a GREAT TEAM... but can the old system be BEAT?? No... not without YOUR participation... RADICAL social change begins on the STREET!! So if you're looking for some ACTION... CUT THE CRAP and GET OUT THERE   (DIRTY PUNK).

(Author's Notes) I'm not sure if no one liked this album or if no one wanted to like this album — there is a difference. The Clash without Mick seemed a little bit like The Beatles without Lennon. On some levels it works. 'This Is England' is one of the finest songs I've ever heard, but some of these songs sound like The Cockney Rejects and from this group that just won't do. Happily, years later whenever The Clash came up in conversation or on television, this album was erased from memory, wiped away like it never existed — which won't upset too many people.

"A good guitar solo in the right place, a little bit of tension added to the show — there's nothing wrong with having respect for the stage, because you're also out there entertaining."
(Mick Jones)

UNCUT

FREE
18-TRACK
CD

A RIOT OF THEIR OWN

THE CLASH

The revolution starts here!

8 MILES HIGH
Eminem conquers Hollywood

SPEED, FEEDBACK AND ZE
How Hüsker Dü changed American rock

COMEDY AND COCAINE
The wild times of Richard Pryor

FRIGHT CLUB
David Cronenberg's world of terro

THE OLD DEVIL
The unstoppable Jack Nicholson

FEBRUARY 2003 £3.90 www.uncut.

9 771368 072060
02

(8) SUPER BLACK MARKET CLASH

COLUMBIA RECORDS 495352 2

(RUNNING TIME: 72 MINUTES 24 SECONDS)
DECEMBER 1993.

1977
LISTEN
JAIL GUITAR DOORS
THE CITY OF THE DEAD
THE PRISONER
PRESSURE DROP
I-2 CRUSH ON YOU
GROOVY TIMES
GATES OF THE WEST
CAPITOL RADIO TWO
TIME IS TIGHT

JUSTICE TONIGHT/KICK IT OVER
ROBBER DUB
THE COOL OUT
STOP THE WORLD
THE MAGNIFICENT DANCE
THIS IS RADIO CLASH
FIRST NIGHT BACK IN LONDON
LONG TIME JERK
COOL CONFUSION
MUSTAPHA DANCE

This collection of songs was issued on CD as a tidy up to all the previous releases, a 10" vinyl album (released 26th August 1991 here in the UK) titled 'Black Market Clash' had been issued some years earlier (1980) which featured the tracks: Capitol Radio One/The Prisoner/Pressure Drop/Cheat/City Of The Dead/Time Is Tight/Bank Robber/Robber Dub/Armagideon Time/Justice Tonight/Kick It Over.

"I don't believe in guitar heroes. If I walk out to the front of the stage it's because I wanna reach the audience, I want to communicate with them. I don't want them to suck my guitar off."
(Mick Jones)

(9) THE STORY OF THE CLASH VOLUME I

COLUMBIA RECORDS 495351 2
MARCH 1988.

(RUNNING TIME DISC ONE: 49 MINUTES)
(RUNNING TIME DISC TWO: 50 MINUTES)

The Story Of THE CLASH

Volume 1

(DISC ONE)
THE MAGNIFICENT SEVEN*
ROCK THE CASBAH*
SHOULD I STAY OR SHOULD I GO*
STRAIGHT TO HELL*
ARMAGIDEON TIME
CLAMPDOWN
TRAIN IN VAIN*
GUNS OF BRIXTON*
I FOUGHT THE LAW*
SOMEBODY GOT MURDERED
LOST IN A SUPERMARKET
BANKROBBER*

(DISC TWO)
(WHITE MAN) IN HAMMERSMITH PALAIS*
LONDON'S BURNING
JANIE JONES
TOMMY GUN*
COMPLETE CONTROL*
CAPITOL RADIO (WITH NME INTERVIEW)*
WHITE RIOT*
CAREER OPPORTUNITIES
CLASH CITY ROCKERS*
SAFE EUROPEAN HOME
STAY FREE
LONDON CALLING*
SPANISH BOMBS
ENGLISH CIVIL WAR*
POLICE & THIEVES

The first proper Clash compilation album containing singles and classic album tracks. A double vinyl version was issued at the same time. The songs which were UK singles are marked * for this listing.

"It's the only thing that's living to me. I shall live and die and be judged by it."
(Joe Strummer talks about rock n' roll)

Free CD!

UNCUT

MUSIC, MOVIES & BOOKS

SEPTEMBER 1999 £2.9

THE CLASH

JOE STRUMMER brings back the glory days

EXCLUSIVE INTERVIEW

The legend of Gram Parsons

The Blue Meanies are back

Bruddas-in-arms

Welcome to the underworld

Plus **IKE TURNER**

GEORGE P PELECANOS

DOUG LIMAN

PAUL AUSTER

9 771368 072039

(10) THE SINGLES

COLUMBIA RECORDS   495353 2

(RUNNING TIME: 64 MINUTES 53 SECONDS)
1991.

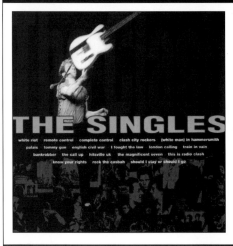

WHITE RIOT
REMOTE CONTROL
COMPLETE CONTROL
CLASH CITY ROCKERS
(WHITE MAN) IN HAMMERSMITH
PALAIS
TOMMY GUN
ENGLISH CIVIL WAR
I FOUGHT THE LAW
LONDON CALLING

TRAIN IN VAIN
BANKROBBER
THE CALL UP
HITSVILLE UK
THE MAGNIFICENT SEVEN
THIS IS RADIO CLASH
KNOW YOUR RIGHTS
ROCK THE CASBAH
SHOULD I STAY OR SHOULD I GO

Yes, it does exactly what it says on the tin! A collection of Clash singles.

"I read everything that TE Lawrence wrote, he was my hero."
(Joe Strummer)

(11) FROM HERE TO ETERNITY (LIVE)

COLUMBIA RECORDS   496183 2

(RUNNING TIME: 63 MINUTES 48 SECONDS)
1999.

(Author's Notes)
At last a live album from The Clash. Compiled by Mick, Joe and Paul, it features songs culled from 9 different gigs. Topper Headon plays drums on all songs marked ^ while all other drumming on this album is by Terry Chimes. Mikey Dread (additional vocals) and Mickey Gallagher (organ) are featured on Armagideon Time.

"I ain't gonna fuck myself up like I seen those other guys fuck themselves up. Keeping all their money for themselves and getting into their heads, and thinking they're the greatest. I've planned what I'm gonna do with my money if it happens. Secret plans."
(Joe Strummer)

COMPLETE CONTROL	recorded at Bonds Casino New York USA (June 13th 1981)^
LONDON'S BURNING	recorded at Victoria Park London UK (April 30th 1978)^
WHAT'S MY NAME	recorded at Music Machine London UK (July 27th 1978)^
CLASH CITY ROCKERS	recorded at The Orpheum Boston USA (September 7th 1982)
CAREER OPPORTUNITIES	recorded at Shea Stadium New York USA (October 13th 1982)
(WHITE MAN) IN HAMMERSMITH PALAIS	recorded at The Orpheum Boston USA (September 7th 1982)
CAPITOL RADIO	recorded at Lewisham Odeon London UK (February 8th 1980)^
CITY OF THE DEAD	recorded at The Lyceum London UK (December 28th 1978)^
I FOUGHT THE LAW	recorded at The Lyceum London UK (December 28th 1978)^
LONDON CALLING	recorded at The Orpheum Boston USA (September 7th 1982)
ARMAGIDEON TIME	recorded at Lewisham Odeon London UK (February 8th 1980)^
TRAIN IN VAIN	recorded at Bonds Casino New York USA (June 13th 1981)^
GUNS OF BRIXTON	recorded at Bonds Casino New York USA (June 13th 1981)^
THE MAGNIFICENT SEVEN	recorded at The Orpheum Boston USA (September 7th 1982)
KNOW YOUR RIGHTS	recorded at The Orpheum Boston USA (September 7th 1982)
SHOULD I STAY OR SHOULD I GO	recorded at The Orpheum Boston USA (September 8th 1982)
STRAIGHT TO HELL	recorded at The Orpheum Boston USA (September 8th 1982)

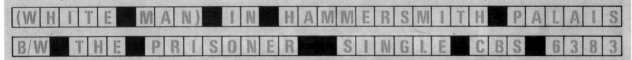

(WHITE MAN) IN HAMMERSMITH PALAIS
B/W THE PRISONER · SINGLE · CBS 6383

THE CLASH

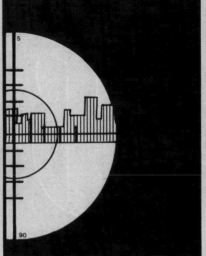

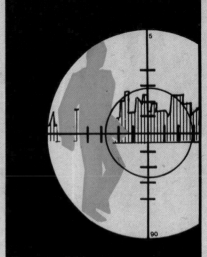

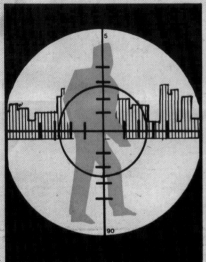

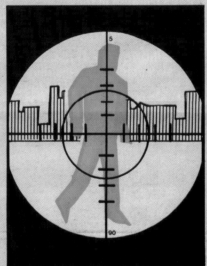

CLASH 'OUT ON PAROLE'

June
28th Friars Aylesbury
29th Queens Hall, Leeds
30th Top Rank, Sheffield

July
1st   Granby Hall, Leicester
2nd   Apollo, Manchester
4th   Apollo, Glasgow
5th   The Music Hall, Aberdeen
6th   Kinema, Dunfermline
8th   Sports Centre, Crawley
9th   Locarno, Bristol
10th Town Hall, Torquay
11th Top Rank, Cardiff
12th Top Rank, Birmingham
13th Empire, Liverpool
14th Corn Exchange,
      Bury St. Edmunds

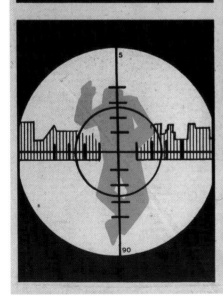

SHOOT OUT

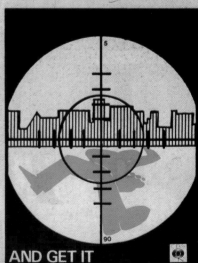

AND GET IT

Left to right: Topper Headon, Paul Simonon, Mick Jones and Joe Strummer Photo: L J van Houten Rex features

The Clash 1981 Photo: Rex features

EPIC/LEGACY RECORDS   497453 2
MAY 1991.

(RUNNING TIME DISC ONE: 67 MINUTES
(RUNNING TIME DISC TWO: 72 MINUTES
(RUNNING TIME DISC THREE: 76 MINUTES

CLASH ON BROADWAY

This three disc collection.
including for the first time
unreleased material, was issued
first in a long box format and
later in a standard square box.
Both versions include a lyric
book, along with a book of
personal interviews with Mick,
Joe and Paul, plus many rare and
previously unseen photographs.

Clash on Broadway Poster

(DISC ONE)
JANIE JONES/DEMO
CAREER OPPORTUNITIES/DEMO
WHITE RIOT
1977
I'M SO BORED WITH THE USA
HATE & WAR
WHAT'S MY NAME
DENY
LONDON'S BURNING
PROTEX BLUE
POLICE & THIEVES
48 HOURS
CHEAT
GARAGELAND
CAPITOL RADIO ONE
COMPLETE CONTROL
CLASH CITY ROCKERS
CITY OF THE DEAD
JAIL GUITAR DOORS
THE PRISONER
(WHITE MAN) IN HAMMERSMITH
PALAIS
PRESSURE DROP
1-2 CRUSH ON YOU
ENGLISH CIVIL WAR/LIVE AT THE
LYCEUM BALLROOM LONDON (1979)
I FOUGHT THE LAW/LIVE FROM 'RUDE
BOY' MOVIE MASTER RECORDING

(DISC TWO)
SAFE EUROPEAN HOME
TOMMY GUN
JULIE'S BEEN WORKING FOR THE
DRUG SQUAD
STAY FREE
ONE EMOTION/PREVIOUSLY
UNRELEASED
GROOVY TIMES

GATES OF THE WEST
ARMAGIDEON TIME
LONDON CALLING
BRAND NEW CADILLAC
RUDIE CAN'T FAIL
THE GUNS OF BRIXTON
SPANISH BOMBS
LOST IN A SUPERMARKET
THE RIGHT PROFILE
THE CARD CHEAT
DEATH OR GLORY
CLAMPDOWN
TRAIN IN VAIN
BANKROBBER

(DISC THREE)
POLICE ON MY BACK
THE MAGNIFICENT SEVEN
THE LEADER
THE CALL UP
SOMEBODY GOT MURDERED
WASHINGTON BULLETS
BROADWAY
LIGHTNING STRIKES (NOT ONCE BUT
TWICE)/LIVE AT BONDS CASINO NEW
YORK (1981)
EVERY LITTLE BIT
HURTS/PREVIOUSLY UNRELEASED
STOP THE WORLD
MIDNIGHT TO STEVENS/PREVIOUSLY
UNRELEASED
THIS IS RADIO CLASH
COOL CONFUSION
RED ANGEL DRAGNET/EDITED VERSION
GHETTO DEFENDANT/EDITED VERSION
ROCK THE CASBAH
SHOULD I STAY OR SHOULD I GO
STRAIGHT TO HELL/UNEDITED VERSION

"I always wanted to be a guitarist, not a bass player, but because I couldn't play
nothing — I just used to leap about with it and not hit any right notes.
So in the end I thought I'll be the bass player —
but I'll be the best bass player"

(Paul Simonon)

COLUMBIA RECORDS 5I09982
IOTH MARCH 2003.

(DISC ONE RUNNING TIME: 6I MINUTES)
(DISC TWO RUNNING TIME: 77 MINUTES)

"While we were compiling this album we suffered the tragic and untimely loss of our friend and collaborator Joe Strummer.
We would like to dedicate this album to his memory."
(Mick Jones & Paul Simonon)

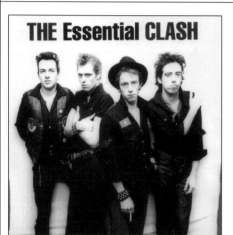

Back cover of The Essential CLASH

(DISC ONE)
WHITE RIOT
1977
LONDON'S BURNING
COMPLETE CONTROL
CLASH CITY ROCKERS
I'M SO BORED WITH THE USA
CAREER OPPORTUNITIES
HATE & WAR
CHEAT
POLICE & THIEVES
JANIE JONES
GARAGELAND
CAPITOL RADIO
(WHITE MAN) IN HAMMERSMITH
PALAIS
ENGLISH CIVIL WAR
TOMMY GUN
SAFE EUROPEAN HOME
JULIE'S BEEN WORKING FOR THE
DRUG SQUAD
STAY FREE
GROOVY TIMES
I FOUGHT THE LAW

(DISC TWO)
LONDON CALLING
GUNS OF BRIXTON
CLAMPDOWN
RUDIE CAN'T FAIL
LOST IN A SUPERMARKET
JIMMY JAZZ
TRAIN IN VAIN
BANKROBBER
MAGNIFICENT SEVEN
IVAN MEETS GI JOE
STOP THE WORLD
SOMEBODY GOT MURDERED
STREET PARADE
BROADWAY
RADIO CLASH
GHETTO DEFENDANT
ROCK THE CASBAH
STRAIGHT TO HELL
SHOULD I STAY OR SHOULD I GO
THIS IS ENGLAND

This collection was released on the very same day that The Clash received their entry into The Rock & Roll Hall Of Fame, over in New York USA. The sleevenotes are from Mojo editor and Clash fan Pat Gilbert. It works perfectly as a collection, but only really for people owning little or none of the aforementioned. The possibility of releasing material from the vaults remains unexplored.
The project was also TV advertised.

"Our response was, what do you mean second album?
It took so much out of us making the first."
(Joe Strummer)

TWO IMPORTANT UK PROMOS:

(1) CLASH ON BROADWAY THE INTERVIEWS

EPIC/LEGACY RECORDS   ESK4337   (RUNNING TIME: 74 MINUTES 27 SECONDS) 1991.

Interviews by Kosmo Vinyl. Mick Jones & Joe Strummer were interviewed in New York City USA in October 1991, while Paul Simonon was interviewed in London UK during November 1991. All songs are same versions as those featured on the Clash On Broadway box set...

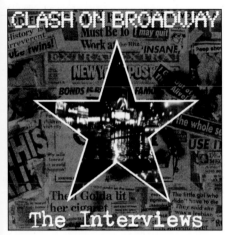

"I was the dark horse of The Clash. If anybody had ever said to me, in an interview, 'What do you do with your spare time?' maybe I'd have turned around and given them a big art lecture. But I think they thought I was an idiot... a thicko from south London."
(Paul Simonon)

MICK JONES
JOE STRUMMER
MICK JONES
PAUL SIMONON
MICK JONES
PAUL SIMONON
JOE STRUMMER
MICK JONES
JOE STRUMMER
MICK JONES
WHITE RIOT
PAUL SIMONON/JOE STRUMMER/
MICK JONES/JOE STRUMMER
COMPLETE CONTROL
MICK JONES/JOE STRUMMER
(WHITE MAN) IN HAMMERSMITH
PALAIS
JOE STRUMMER
JULIE'S BEEN WORKING FOR THE
DRUG SQUAD
PAUL SIMONON/JOE STRUMMER
ONE EMOTION
JOE STRUMMER/MICK JONES
I FOUGHT THE LAW/LIVE

MICK JONES/PAUL SIMONON/
JOE STRUMMER
LONDON CALLING
JOE STRUMMER/MICK JONES
LOST IN A SUPERMARKET
PAUL SIMONON
THE GUNS OF BRIXTON
PAUL SIMONON/MICK JONES
TRAIN IN VAIN
JOE STRUMMER
ROCK THE CASBAH
MICK JONES/JOE STRUMMER/
PAUL SIMONON
SHOULD I STAY OR SHOULD I GO
PAUL SIMONON/MICK JONES/
JOE STRUMMER
EVERY LITTLE BIT HURTS
MICK JONES/PAUL SIMONON/
JOE STRUMMER

(2) ROCKERS GALORE

EPIC/LEGACY RECORDS   ESK47144   (RUNNING TIME: 62 MINUTES 49 SECONDS) 1999.

COMPLETE CONTROL/LIVE
PAUL SIMONON
MICK JONES
JOE STRUMMER
MICK
JANIE JONES
PAUL
WHITE RIOT
TOPPER HEADON
TOMMY GUN
PAUL & MICK
TRAIN IN VAIN

PAUL
GUNS OF BRIXTON
PAUL
ROCKERS GALORE
MICK
THE MAGNIFICENT SEVEN
JOE
POLICE ON MY BACK
JOE
ROCK THE CASBAH
JOE
STRAIGHT TO HELL/LIVE

Released to tie in with the complete re-issue of all The Clash albums on CD, this disc contains several songs and interviews, it was the first time ever that the song 'Rockers Galore' had ever seen the light of day on CD...

CLASH CRIMINAL RECORDS:

THE CLASH

(JUNE 1977)
Joe Strummer and Topper Headon fined five pounds for spraying the word 'Clash' on the wall at Dingwalls in Camden, London.

Joe Strummer and Topper Headon detained overnight because they fail to appear in court up in Newcastle, after stealing pillow cases. They are fined one hundred pounds.

(MARCH 1978)
Paul Simonon and Topper Headon arrested in Camden, London for shooting racing pigeons with air guns. They get an eight hundred pound fine.

(JULY 1978)
Joe Strummer and Paul Simonon fined for being drunk and disorderly after a gig in Glasgow at the notorious Apollo.

(MAY 1978)
Joe Strummer arrested after smashing his guitar over a violent fan's head in Hamburg.

(DECEMBER 1981)
Topper Headon caught at London's Heathrow Airport, smuggling heroin.

(JULY 1982)
Topper Headon remanded on bail in London, charged with stealing a bus stop and receiving stolen property.

"We love the place - blocks of flats, concrete. I hate the country. The minute I see cows I get sick."
(Joe Strummer talks about London)

UK 7" SINGLES.

All the following singles were released on the CBS Records label, except those marked * they all came in picture sleeves, and are all listed with catalogue order numbers and release dates:

WHITE RIOT/1977   CBS 5058   (released 18th March 1977)

CAPITOL RADIO/NME INTERVIEW/LISTEN   NME FREEBIE   (released 9th April 1977)*

REMOTE CONTROL/LONDON'S BURNING (LIVE)   CBS 5293   (released 13th May 1977)

COMPLETE CONTROL/CITY OF THE DEAD   CBS 5664   (released 23rd September 1977)

CLASH CITY ROCKERS/JAIL GUITAR DOORS   CBS 5834   (released 17th February 1978)

WHITE MAN IN HAMMERSMITH PALAIS/THE PRISONER   CBS 6383   (released 16th June 1978)

TOMMY GUN/1-2 CRUSH ON YOU   CBS 6788   (released 24th November 1978)

ENGLISH CIVIL WAR/PRESSURE DROP   CBS 7082   (released 23rd February 1979)

THE COST OF LIVING (EP) I FOUGHT THE LAW/   CBS 7324   (released 11th May 1979)
GROOVY TIMES/GATES OF THE WEST/CAPITOL RADIO

LONDON CALLING/ARMAGIDEON TIME   CBS 8087   (released 7th December 1979)

BANKROBBER/ROCKERS GALORE   CBS 8323   (released 8th August 1980)

THE CALL UP/STOP THE WORLD   CBS 9339   (released 21st November 1980)

HITSVILLE UK/ RADIO ONE   CBS 9480   (released 16th January 1981)

THE MAGNIFICENT SEVEN/THE MAGNIFICENT DANCE   CBS A 1133   (released 10th April 1981)
ALSO RELEASED IN 12" FORMAT

THIS IS RADIO CLASH/RADIO CLASH   CBS A 1797   (released 20th November 1981)
ALSO RELEASED IN 12" FORMAT

KNOW YOUR RIGHTS/FIRST NIGHT BACK IN LONDON   CBS A 2309   (released 23rd April 1982)
CAME WITH FREE STICKER 'THE FUTURE IS UNWRITTEN'

ROCK THE CASBAH/LONG TIME JERK   CBS A 2479   (released 11th June 1982)
CAME WITH SHEET OF 4 STICKERS.
WAS ALSO ISSUED IN 12" AND PICTURE DISC 7"

STRAIGHT TO HELL/SHOULD I STAY OR SHOULD I GO   CBS A 2646   (released 17th September 1982)
CAME WITH A FREE STICKER.
WAS ALSO ISSUED IN 12" (WHICH INCLUDED CLASH STENCIL)
AND A PICTURE DISC 7"

THIS IS ENGLAND/DO IT NOW   CBS A 6122   (released 14th September 1985)
CAME WITH A POSTER SLEEVE.
ALSO IN 12" FORMAT AND A 7" PICTURE DISC

TWO IMPORTANT USA CD ALBUMS

These two albums appeared on CD over 2 years, they came officially from CBS via Relativity Music. Both are quite hard to find now.

(1) CRUCIAL MUSIC: THE CLASH COLLECTION

1989   88561- 1036- 2   (RUNNING TIME: 24 MINUTES 49 SECONDS)

CLASH CITY ROCKERS
POLICE & THIEVES
TOMMY GUN
STAY FREE
SAFE EUROPEAN HOME
TRAIN IN VAIN
CLAMPDOWN
MAGNIFICENT SEVEN
POLICE ON MY BACK
STRAIGHT TO HELL

(2) CRUCIAL MUSIC: A COLLECTION OF RARE TRACKS AND B SIDES

1990   88561- 1036- 2   (RUNNING TIME: 24 MINUTES 49 SECONDS)

1977
LONDON'S BURNING
DENY
CHEAT
48 HOURS
PROTEX BLUE
GROOVY TIMES
GATES OF THE WEST
1-2 CRUSH ON YOU
STOP THE WORLD

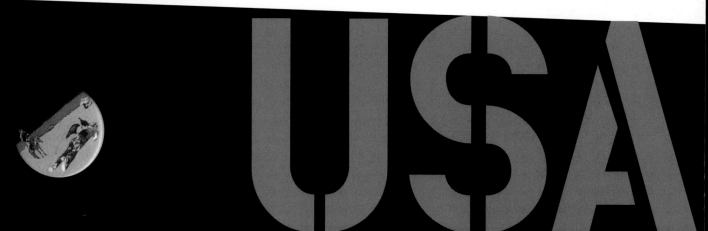

UK DVD GUIDE

(1) WESTWAY TO THE WORLD

SMV ENTERPRISES 201510 9 (RELEASE 2001) CERTIFICATE 15

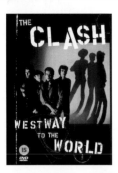

Don Letts' excellent documentary of The Clash and one of the best rock documentaries ever. This disc features a full director's cut of the movie (running roughly 90 minutes), plus a decent selection of bonus footage, which includes: Clash On Broadway, previously unseen USA footage from the groups personal collection, largely filmed around the Bonds Casino gigs in New York City. Exclusive unseen interview footage. A photo gallery. Full discography. Subtitles in English, Spanish and French. With full interactive menu, the DVD is available digitally mastered in PCM stereo.

WWW.WESTWAYTOTHEWORLD.COM

(2) RUDE BOY

METRODOME DISTRIBUTION LTD MTD5053 (RELEASE 2001) CERTIFICATE 18

The original Clash movie in its full 127 minute cut, the bonus footage on this disc includes: English Civil War & White Riot performed live, production notes from original cast production book.
Image library, Animated and Scored graphics.

(3) PUNK IN LONDON

METRODOME DISTRIBUTION LTD MTD5061 (RELEASE 2001) CERTIFICATE EXEMPT

The full story of punk in London, which along with The Clash features performances from; The Adverts, X-Ray Spex, Subway Sect, The Boomtown Rats, The Jam, Chelsea, Wayne County And The Electric Chairs. The main feature running time is 84 minutes, but the bonus footage includes never before seen footage of The Clash live in Munich (and The Adverts live in Berlin).

WWW.PUNKBOOK.COM

(4) THE ESSENTIAL CLASH

SMV ENTERPRISES 201886 9 (RELEASE 2003) CERTIFICATE 15

A compilation of promo videos and lost footage, featuring: Clash On Broadway (movie trailer)/White Riot/Complete Control/Tommy Gun/Clampdown/Train In Vain/London Calling/Bankrobber/The Call Up/Rock The Casbah/Should I Stay Or Should I Go/Career Opportunities/Hell W10 (short movie directed by Joe Strummer in 1983)/Promo footage from 1976/I Fought The Law/Interview: London Weekend Show 1976.

"We don't walk around with green hair and bondage trousers anymore. We just want to look, sort of, flash these days."
(Joe Strummer)

FULL CLASH UK GIG LISTING
1976 TILL 1984

(1976)

4TH JULY	BLACK SWAN	Sheffield
13TH AUGUST*	REHEARSALS REHEARSALS	Camden Town, London
29TH AUGUST	SCREEN ON THE GREEN	London
31ST AUGUST	100 CLUB	London
5TH SEPTEMBER	THE ROUNDHOUSE	Camden Town, London

*Private gig/invite only
(All the above gigs were played with a 5 piece line up featuring future Public Image Limited guitarist Keith Levene)

"I remember just feeling terrified, standing there with all these mad looking punk rockers, not knowing what was about to happen. The guy next to me screamed 'Come On' and Joe appeared on stage. The place went crazy. I'd never seen anything like it before. I've been to see a thousand bands since and nothing comes close to them live, nothing."

(Sean/Clash fan)

20TH SEPTEMBER*	100 CLUB	London
9TH OCTOBER	TINDERFOOT LEISURE CENTRE	Leyton Buzzard
15TH OCTOBER	ACKLAM HALL	Ladbroke Grove, London
16TH OCTOBER	UNIVERSITY OF LONDON	London
23RD OCTOBER	INSTITUTE OF CONTEMPORARY ARTS	London
27TH OCTOBER	BARBARELLAS	Birmingham
29TH OCTOBER	TOWN HALL	Fulham, London
5TH NOVEMBER**	ROYAL COLLEGE OF ART	London
11TH NOVEMBER	LADY LADY	Ilford
18TH NOVEMBER	NAG'S HEAD	High Wycombe
29TH NOVEMBER	LANCASTER POLYTECHNIC	Coventry

* as part of the club's two day punk festival
** billed as 'A Night Of Treason'

"I saw The Clash in Florence, Italy in May 1981. A lot of time has passed since but I clearly remember them entering the stage to the noise of Morricone's music and then... two hours of hell. Furious mosh-pitting and an unforgettable show."

(David/Clash fan)

(1976)

6TH DECEMBER	POLYTECHNIC	Leeds
9TH DECEMBER	ELECTRIC CIRCUS	Manchester
14TH DECEMBER	CASTLE CINEMA	Caerphilly, Wales
19TH DECEMBER	ELECTRIC CIRCUS	Manchester
20TH DECEMBER	WINTER GARDENS	Cleethorpes
21ST DECEMBER	WOODS CENTRE	Plymouth
22ND DECEMBER	WOODS CENTRE	Plymouth

"All that business on the Pistols tour! I hated it. I HATED it. It was the Pistols time. We were in the background. The first few nights were terrible. We were just locked up in the hotel room with the Pistols doing nothing."
(Joe Strummer)

These December shows represent all that was actually played on the ill-fated Sex Pistols 'Anarchy' Tour after several councils withdrew entertainment licences, thus cancelling shows nationwide.

"The sirens. The barriers go up and down and then they're on. One more time - MUST I GET A WITNESS? Then they would see the magic powers of favourite cartoon characters; the stage-destroying pneumatic leg, the bassman's bullet-dodging twitch, the guitarist's skyscraper clearing glam rock leap and the earthquake maker on the riser. Politics and poetry."
(Ben/Clash fan)

(1977)

1ST JANUARY	THE ROXY	Covent Garden, London
11TH MARCH	COLISSEUM	Harlesden, London
1ST MAY	CIVIC HALL	Guildford
2ND MAY	RASCALS	Chester
3RD MAY	BARBARELLAS	Birmingham
4TH MAY	AFFAIR	Swindon
5TH MAY	ERIC'S	Liverpool
6TH MAY	UNIVERSITY	Aberdeen
7TH MAY	PLAYHOUSE	Edinburgh
8TH MAY	ELECTRIC CIRCUS	Manchester
9TH MAY	RAINBOW	London
10TH MAY	TOWN HALL	Kidderminster
12TH MAY	PALAIS	Nottingham
13TH MAY	POLYTECHNIC	Leicester
15TH MAY	FIESTA	Plymouth
16TH MAY	UNIVERSITY	Swansea
17TH MAY	POLYTECHNIC	Leeds
19TH MAY	ROCK GARDEN	Middlesbrough
20TH MAY	UNIVERSITY	Newcastle

21ST MAY	CITY HALL	St Albans
22ND MAY	SKINDLES	Maidenhead
23RD MAY	TOP OF THE WORLD	Stafford
24TH MAY	TOP RANK	Cardiff
25TH MAY	POLYTECHNIC	Brighton
26TH MAY	COLSTON	Bristol
27TH MAY	PAVILION	West Runton
28TH MAY	ODEON	Canterbury
29TH MAY	CHANCELLOR	Chelmsford
30TH MAY	CALIFORNIA	Dunstable

(All the above May dates represent the 'White Riot' Tour)

"I am only 18. I have never seen The Clash but I would sell my grandmother to have seen them."
(David/Clash fan)

20TH OCTOBER	ULSTER HALL	Belfast
21ST OCTOBER	TRINITY COLLEGE	Dublin
24TH OCTOBER	KINEMA	Dunfermline
25TH OCTOBER	APOLLO	Glasgow
26TH OCTOBER	CLOUDS	Edinburgh
27TH OCTOBER	UNIVERSITY	Leeds
28TH OCTOBER	POLYTECHNIC	Newcastle
29TH OCTOBER	APOLLO	Manchester
30TH OCTOBER	VICTORIA	Stoke
1ST NOVEMBER	TOP RANK	Sheffield
2ND NOVEMBER	UNIVERSITY	Bradford
3RD NOVEMBER	KINGS HALL	Derby
4TH NOVEMBER	UNIVERSITY	Cardiff
6TH NOVEMBER	MARKET HALL	Carlisle
7TH NOVEMBER	TOP RANK	Birmingham
8TH NOVEMBER	LOCARNO	Coventry
9TH NOVEMBER	WINTER GARDENS	Bournemouth
10TH NOVEMBER	EXHIBITION CENTRE	Bristol
11TH NOVEMBER	CORN EXCHANGE	Cambridge
12TH NOVEMBER	PAVILION	Hastings
13TH NOVEMBER	TOP RANK	Southampton

(All shows in October/November represent the 'Out Of Control' Tour)

13TH DECEMBER	RAINBOW	London
14TH DECEMBER	RAINBOW	London
15TH DECEMBER	RAINBOW	London

Postcard: Paul, Mick & Topper

MAKING YOU A BETTER BASS PLAYER

bassist

The CLASH

INTERVIEW & TECHNIQUE!

Paul Simonon's first ever bass interview PLUS: play London Calling and more

25 YEARS OF THE STRANGLERS

JJ Burnel looks back over two and a half decades of bass abuse

BILLY SHEEHAN chooses his top bass albums

YES

Bass giant Chris Squire on the making of the new album

NEW! Our guide to the best kit of the last six months

future
Your Guarantee Of Value

NOVEMBER 1999

£3.25

9 771355 775073

"It's easier when there's no spit on the guitar - it gets slippery. The only people who gob in England are up north - they're a bit behind."
(Mick Jones)

(1978)

| 30TH APRIL | VICTORIA PARK | London |

('Rock Against Racism' show, included appearance by Jimmy Pursey of Sham 69 during The Clash set)

"Here they have a tendency to lay money on the stage instead of gobbing. I made 17 dollars the other day - it's great!"
(Paul Simonon)

28TH JUNE	FRIARS	Aylesbury
29TH JUNE	QUEENS HALL	Leeds
30TH JUNE	TOP RANK	Sheffield
1ST JULY	GRANBY HALL	Leicester
2ND JULY	APOLLO	Manchester
4TH JULY	APOLLO	Glasgow
5TH JULY	MUSIC HALL	Aberdeen
6TH JULY	LEISURE CENTRE	Chester
8TH JULY	SPORTS CENTRE	Crawley
9TH JULY	LOCARNO	Bristol
10TH JULY	TOWN HALL	Torquay
11TH JULY	TOP RANK	Cardiff
12TH JULY	TOP RANK	Birmingham
24TH JULY	MUSIC MACHINE	London
25TH JULY	MUSIC MACHINE	London
26TH JULY	MUSIC MACHINE	London
27TH JULY	MUSIC MACHINE	London

(All shows in June/July represent the 'Out On Parole' Tour)

"Sometimes the audience would kick in at the same time as the band and you'd think, Christ, this is amazing."
(Pennie Smith)

25TH OCTOBER	ROXY THEATRE	Harlesden, London
26TH OCTOBER	ROXY THEATRE	Harlesden, London
16TH NOVEMBER	ODEON	Edinburgh
17TH NOVEMBER	TOWN HALL	Middlesbrough
18TH NOVEMBER	UNIVERSITY	Leeds
19TH NOVEMBER	TOP RANK	Sheffield

20TH NOVEMBER	DE MONTFORD	Leicester
21ST NOVEMBER	LOCARNO	Bristol
22ND NOVEMBER	VILLAGE BOWL	Bournemouth
23RD NOVEMBER	APOLLO	Manchester
24TH NOVEMBER	KINGS HALL	Derby
26TH NOVEMBER	TOP RANK	Cardiff
27TH NOVEMBER	UNIVERSITY	Exeter
28TH NOVEMBER	TIFFANYS	Coventry
29TH NOVEMBER	VICTORIA HALL	Stoke
30TH NOVEMBER	WIRRANA	Peterborough
2ND DECEMBER	POLYTECHNIC	Newcastle
4TH DECEMBER	UNIVERSITY	Glasgow
5TH DECEMBER	UNIVERSITY	Glasgow
6TH DECEMBER	UNIVERSITY	Liverpool
18TH DECEMBER	TIFFANYS	Purley

(All shows in November/December represent the 'Sort It Out' Tour)

"I saw The Clash for the first time at The Hollywood Palladium in '82. The Clash made me re-invent myself as a better person in society. After that it was girls, The Clash, Art, Movies and Coca Cola My thanks to The Clash for having the balls to rock."

(George/Clash fan)

19TH DECEMBER*	MUSIC MACHINE	London
22ND DECEMBER	FRIARS	Aylesbury
28TH DECEMBER	LYCEUM	London
29TH DECEMBER	LYCEUM	London

* Sid Vicious Defence Fund Benefit

(1979) (1979)

3RD JANUARY	LYCEUM	London

"It ain't punk. It ain't new wave. It's the next step, and the logical progression for groups to move. Call it what you like - all the terms stink. Just call it rock n' roll."

(Mick Jones)

5TH JULY	NOTRE DAME HALL	London (Secret Gigs)
6TH JULY	NOTRE DAME HALL	London (Secret Gigs)
14TH JULY	RAINBOW	London
*25TH DECEMBER	ACKLAM HALL	Ladbroke Grove London
*26TH DECEMBER	ACKLAM HALL	Ladbroke Grove London
27TH DECEMBER	HAMMERSMITH ODEON	London

*Secret Christmas Gigs

"What I saw that night was the most exciting, loud and intense concert I ever saw, and still have ever seen. The Clash came out in bright coloured uniforms and never stopped moving the entire show. They played most of the songs from their not-yet-released debut album and blew the whole audience away"
(Roy/Clash fan)

(1980)

Date	Venue	City
5TH JANUARY	FRIARS	Aylesbury
6TH JANUARY	ODEON	Canterbury
8TH JANUARY	TOP RANK	Brighton
9TH JANUARY	TOP RANK	Brighton
11TH JANUARY	LEISURE CENTRE	Crawley
12TH JANUARY	PAVILLION	Hastings
13TH JANUARY	LOCARNO	Bristol
14TH JANUARY	GAUMONT	Ipswich
16TH JANUARY	DE MONTFORD	Leicester
18TH JANUARY	CAIRD HALL	Dundee
19TH JANUARY	ODEON	Edinburgh
20TH JANUARY	ODEON	Edinburgh
21ST JANUARY	APOLLO	Glasgow
22ND JANUARY	APOLLO	Glasgow
23RD JANUARY	UNIVERSITY	Lancaster
24TH JANUARY	TIFFANYS	Blackpool
25TH JANUARY	KING GEORGES HALL	Blackburn

"About three days after the gig the careers officer came to our school to see those who were due to leave.
'What do you want to do?', she asked me.
'I'm not sure?' I replied, 'but definitely not a real job!'.
I couldn't imagine doing 45 years of anything after January 25th"
(Alan Parker)

Date	Venue	City
26TH JANUARY	LEISURE CENTRE	Chester
27TH JANUARY	TOP RANK	Sheffield
29TH JANUARY	ST GEORGES	Bradford
30TH JANUARY	ROYAL HALL	Bridlington
31ST JANUARY	UNIVERSITY	Leeds
1ST FEBRUARY	VICTORIA HALL	Hanley
3RD FEBRUARY	APOLLO	Manchester
4TH FEBRUARY	APOLLO	Manchester
5TH FEBRUARY	TOP RANK	Birmingham
6TH FEBRUARY	TOP RANK	Birmingham
7TH FEBRUARY	TIFFANYS	Coventry

JOE STRUMMER'S LEATHER JACKET

MICK JONES: LEATHER JACKET

CLOTHING

OPPRESSION

PUNK

HN CALE   CLASH   CRIME

$ STILL 1.00 ONLY

HOLMSTROM '77

DICTATORS

9TH FEBRUARY	GUILDHALL	Portsmouth
10TH FEBRUARY	WESSEX HALL	Poole
11TH FEBRUARY	SOPHIA GARDENS	Cardiff
12TH FEBRUARY	STATE SIDE	Bournemouth
13TH FEBRUARY	TOP RANK	Southampton
15TH FEBRUARY	ELECTRIC BALLROOM	London
16TH FEBRUARY	ELECTRIC BALLROOM	London
17TH FEBRUARY	LYCEUM	London
18TH FEBRUARY	ODEON	Lewisham

(All the above shows made up the 'Sixteen Tons' Tour)

"This stuff about fans staying in our hotel rooms and coming backstage is very important –
the responsibility is to the fans, not only to keep in touch but also to show that we do care,
and I believe that this group cares more than any other in the country."
(Mick Jones)

16TH JUNE	HAMMERSMITH PALAIS	LONDON
17TH JUNE	HAMMERSMITH PALAIS	LONDON

"Same shit different century."
(Joe Strummer)

(1981)

5TH OCTOBER	APOLLO	Manchester
6TH OCTOBER	APOLLO	Manchester
7TH OCTOBER	APOLLO	Glasgow
8TH OCTOBER	APOLLO	Glasgow
10TH OCTOBER	LYCEUM	Sheffield
12TH OCTOBER	ROYAL COURT	Liverpool
15TH OCTOBER	COLISSEUM	St Austell
18TH - 26TH OCTOBER	LYCEUM	London
(no shows on 23rd/24th)		

(All the above shows made up the 'Radio Clash' Tour)

(1982)

(1982)

10TH JULY	FAIR DEAL	Brixton, London
11TH JULY	FAIR DEAL	Brixton, London
12TH JULY	SPORT CENTRE	Stoke
13TH JULY	VICTORIA HALL	Hanley
14TH JULY	CITY HALL	Newcastle
15TH JULY	CITY HALL	Newcastle
17TH JULY	FAIR DEAL	Brixton, London
18TH JULY	BINGLEY HALL	Birmingham
19TH JULY	ASSEMBLY ROOMS	Derby
20TH JULY	DE MONTFORD	Leicester
22ND JULY	LEISURE CENTRE	Irvine
23RD JULY	PLAYHOUSE	Edinburgh
24TH JULY	ICE RINK	Inverness
26TH JULY	UNIVERSITY	Leeds
27TH JULY	ARTS CENTRE	Poole
28TH JULY	GUILDHALL	Portsmouth
30TH JULY	FAIR DEAL	Brixton, London
31ST JULY	FAIR DEAL	Brixton, London
2ND AUGUST	LOCARNO	Bristol
3RD AUGUST	LOCARNO	Bristol

(All the above shows made up the 'Down At The Casbah Club' Tour)

"Punk's now become 'Oh yeah, he's got zips all over him sewed on by his mother and he's shouting in Cockney'."

(Mick Jones)

(1984)

(1984)

5TH FEBRUARY	SFX	Dublin
6TH FEBRUARY	SFX	Dublin
7TH FEBRUARY	ULSTER HALL	Belfast
8TH FEBRUARY	ULSTER HALL	Belfast
10TH FEBRUARY	BARROWLANDS	Glasgow
11TH FEBRUARY	APOLLO	Manchester
12TH FEBRUARY	DE MONTFORD	Leicester
13TH FEBRUARY	COLSTON	Bristol
3RD MARCH	PLAYHOUSE	Edinburgh

2 December 1978   U.S. $1.10c/Canada 80c   20p

NME
NEW MUSICAL EXPRESS

DEVOTO
True Confessions

pages 34-37

PICTURE (NME) by PENNIE SMITH

C·L·A·S·H
pages 25-27

4TH MARCH	KING GEORGES HALL	Blackburn
5TH MARCH	ROYAL COURT	Liverpool
6TH MARCH	GUILDHALL	Portsmouth
8TH MARCH	ACADEMY	Brixton, London
9TH MARCH	ACADEMY	Brixton, London
10TH MARCH	ACADEMY	Brixton, London
12TH MARCH	ULSTER HALL	Belfast
13TH MARCH	SFX	Dublin
14TH MARCH	SFX	Dublin
16TH MARCH	ACADEMY	Brixton, London
17TH MARCH	ACADEMY	Brixton, London

(All the above shows made up the 'Out Of Control 2' Tour)

"People like The Clash always said they wouldn't do it, but... to even be in something as corrupt as the music business is far worse than doing something stupid like Top Of The Pops."
(Pete Wylie)

| 6TH DECEMBER | ACADEMY | Brixton, London |
| 7TH DECEMBER | ACADEMY | Brixton, London |

(Both the above were advertised as 'Scargill's Christmas Party Miner's Benefit Gig' - they represent the last ever UK shows played by The Clash)

"I went to shake The Clash up, to shake The Clash fans up, to shake The Clash haters up, and to shake myself up, too."
(Joe Strummer)

"There are some people who are becoming snobs."
(Mick Jones)

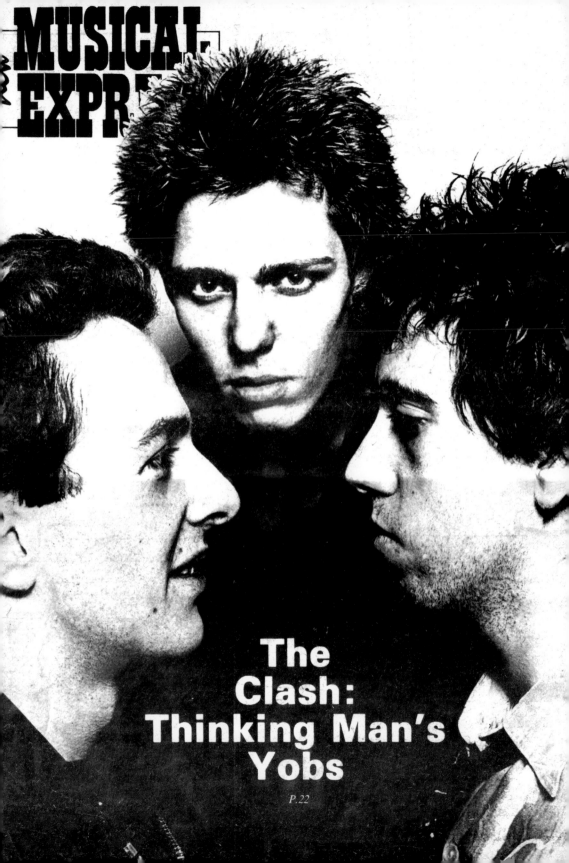

MUSICAL
EXPR

**The
Clash:
Thinking Man's
Yobs**

P.22

BOOTLEG CDS

(All CDs contained in this section of the book have been marked out of 10 for sound quality)

(1) HAMMERSMITH ODEON LONDON DECEMBER 27TH 1979. (RUNNING TIME: 51 MINUTES 4 SECONDS)

CLASH CITY ROCKERS
BRAND NEW CADILLAC
SAFE EUROPEAN HOME
JIMMY JAZZ
CLAMPDOWN
THE GUNS OF BRIXTON
TRAIN IN VAIN
WRONG 'EM BOYO
KOKA KOLA
WHITE MAN IN HAMMERSMITH PALAIS
STAY FREE
BANKROBBER
JANIE JONES

COMPLETE CONTROL
ARMAGIDEON TIME
LONDON CALLING

SOUND: **7**

(2) PALAIS ST SAUVER, FRANCE, MAY 9TH 1981. (RUNNING TIME: 60 MINUTES 13 SECONDS)

LONDON CALLING
SAFE EUROPEAN HOME
THE LEADER
SOMEBODY GOT MURDERED
WHITE MAN IN HAMMERSMITH PALAIS
THE GUNS OF BRIXTON
LIGHTNING STRIKES
I FOUGHT THE LAW
CORNER SOUL
IVAN MEETS GI JOE
THIS IS RADIO CLASH
CHARLIE DON'T SURF
THE MAGNIFICENT SEVEN

BANKROBBER
WRONG 'EM BOYO
TRAIN IN VAIN

SOUND: **8**

(3) BUY OR DIE/LYCEUM LONDON DECEMBER 28TH/29TH 1978. (RUNNING TIME: 72 MINUTES 49 SECONDS)

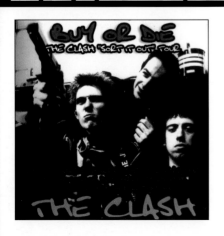

SAFE EUROPEAN HOME
I FOUGHT THE LAW
JAIL GUITAR DOORS
DRUG STABBING TIME
CHEAPSKATES
THE CITY OF THE DEAD
CLASH CITY ROCKERS
TOMMY GUN
WHITE MAN IN HAMMERSMITH PALAIS
ENGLISH CIVIL WAR
STAY FREE
GUNS ON THE ROOF

POLICE & THIEVES
JULIE'S BEEN WORKING FOR THE
DRUG SQUAD
CAPITOL RADIO
JANIE JONES
GARAGELAND
COMPLETE CONTROL
LONDON'S BURNING
WHITE RIOT
ROCKERS GALORE (TAKEN FROM
ORIGINAL B-SIDE OF 'BANKROBBER')

SOUND: **10**

THE ARMAGIDEON TIMES no3

THE MAGNIFICENT SEVEN

RING! RING! ITS SEVEN A.M.!
MOVE Y'SELF TO GO AGAIN
COLD WATER IN THE FACE
 BRINGS YOU BACK TO THIS AWFUL PLACE
KNUCKLE MERCHANTS AND YOU BANKERS TOO,
MUST GET UP-AN LEARN THOSE RULES
WEATHER MAN AND THE CRAZY CHIEF
ONE SAYS SUN AND ONE SAYS SLEET
A.M. THE F.M., THE P.M. TOO
CHURNING OUT THAT BOOGALOO
GETS YOU UP AND GETS YOU OUT
BUT HOW LONG CAN YOU KEEP IT UP?
GIMME HONDA GIMME SONY
SO CHEAP AND REAL PHONY
HONG KONG DOLLARS + INDIAN CENTS
ENGLISH POUNDS & ESKIMO PENCE
YOU LOT! WHAT? DON'T STOP!
 GIVE IT ALL YOU GOT!

WORKING FOR A RISE, BETTER MY STATION
TAKE MY BABY TO SOPHISTICATION
SHE'S SEEN THE AD'S, SHE THINKS ITS NICE
BETTER WORK HARD-I SEEN THE PRICE
NEVER MIND THAT ITS TIME FOR THE BUS
WE GOT TO WORK-AN YOU'RE ONE OF US
CLOCKS GO SLOW IN A PLACE OF WORK
MINUTES DRAG AND THE HOURS JERK
WHEN CAN I TELL 'EM WOT I DO?
IN A SECOND MAAAN... OR IN'T CHUCK!"
WAVE BUB-BUB-BUB BYE TO THE BOSS
ITS OUR PROFIT-ITS HIS LOSS
BUT ANYWAY LUNCH BELLS RING
TAKE 1 HOUR AND DO YOUR THAAANG!
Cheers boiger!
WHAT DO WE HAVE FOR ENTERTAINMENT?
COPS KICKIN' GYPSIES ON THE PAVEMENT
NOW THE NEWS-SNAP TO ATTENTION!
THE LUNAR LANDING of the DENTIST CONVENTION
ITALIAN MOBSTER SHOOTS A LOBSTER
SEA FOOD RESTAURANT GETS OUT OF HAND
A WANNA CAR IN THE FRIDGE
OR A FRIDGE IN THE CAR?
LIKE COWBOYS DO-
 IN T.V. LAND
YOU LOT! WHAT? DON'T S.RQP! HON?
SO GET BACK TO WORK AN SWEAT SOME MORE
THE SUN WILL SINK AN WE'LL GET OUT THE DOOR
IT'S NO GOOD FOR MAN TO WORK IN CAGES
HITS THE TOWN, HE DRINKS HIS WAGES
YOU'RE FRETTIN' YOU'RE SWEATIN'
DID YOU NOTICE YOU AINT GETTIN'?
DON'T YOU EVER STOP LONG ENOUGH TO START
TO GET YOUR CAR OUTTA THAT GEAR?
KARLO MARX AND FREDRICH ENGELS
CAME TO THE CHECKOUT AT THE 7-11
MARX WAS SKINT-BUT HE HAD SENSE
ENGELS LENT HIM THE NECESSARY PENCE
WHAT HAVE WE GOT? YEN-O, MAGNIFICENCE!
LUTHER KING AND MAHATMA GANDHI
WENT TO THE PARK TO CHECK ON THE BALL
BUT THEY WAS MURDERED BY THE OTHER TEAM
WHO WENT ON TO WIN - 50 - NIL
YOU CAN BE TRUE, YOU CAN BE FALSE
YOU BE GIVEN THE SAME REWARD
SOCRATES AND MILHOUS NIXON
BOTH WENT THE SAME WAY-THRU THE KITCHEN
PLATO THE GREEK OR RIN-TIN-TIN?
WHO'S MORE FAMOUS TO THE BILLION MILLION?
FLASH! VACUUM CLEANER SUCKS UP BUDGIE
BUB-BUB-BYE! MAGNIFICENCE!!

HITSVILLE U.K.

THEY CRIED THE TEARS, THEY SHED THE FEARS,
 UP AND DOWN THE LAND,
THEY STOLE GUITARS OR USED GUITARS
 - SO THE TAPE WOULD UNDERSTAND,
WITHOUT EVEN THE SLIGHTEST HOPE OF A 1,000 SALES
JUST AS IF, AS IF THERE WAS, A HITSVILLE IN U.K.,
I KNOW THE BOY WAS ALL ALONE, TIL THE HITSVILLE HIT U.K.

THEY SAY TRUE TALENT WILL ALLWAYS EMERGE IN TIME,
WHEN LIGHTENING HITS SMALL WONDER-
 ITS FAST ROUGH FACTORY TRADE,
NO EXPENSE ACCOUNTS, OR LUNCH DISCOUNTS
 OR HYPEING UP THE CHARTS,
THE BAND WENT IN, 'N KNOCKED 'EM DEAD, IN 2 MIN.59.

- NO SLIMY DEALS, WITH SMARMY EELS- IN HITSVILLE U.K.
LETS SHAKE 'N SAY, WE'LL OPERATE - IN HITSVILLE U.K.
THE MUTANTS, CREEPS AND MUSCLE MEN,
ARE SHAKING LIKE A LEAF,
IT BLOWS A HOLE IN THE RADIO,
WHEN IT HASNT SOUNDED GOOD ALL WEEK,
 A MIKE 'N BOOM, IN YOUR LIVING ROOM - IN HITSVILLE U.K.
NO CONSUMER TRIALS, OR A.O.R. - IN HITSVILLE U.K.,
NOW THE BOYS AND GIRLS ARE NOT ALONE,
 NOW THE HITSVILLE'S HIT U.K.

JUNCO PARTNER (WRITER, AT PRESENT, UNKNOWN)

DOWN THE ROAD CAME A JUNCO
BOY HE WAS LOADED AS DRUNK
HE WAS KNOCKED OUT LOADED
HE WAS WOBBLING
 ALL OVER THE STREET

SIX AND SIX MONTHS AN NO
 SENTENCE
YEH AND 1 YEAR AINT NO TIME
I WAS BORN
 IN ANGOLA
SERVING FOURTEEN
 TO NINETY-NINE

WELL I WISH I HAD ME
 1,000,000 DOLLARS
JUST ONE MILLION
 TO CALL MY OWN
I WOULD RAISE ME
 A TOBACCO FARM

WHEN I HAD ME
 A GREAT DEAL OF MONEY
HAD MIGHTY GOOD FRIENDS
 ALL OVER TOWN
BUT NOW I AINT GOT
 NO MORE MONEY
ALL OF MY GOOD FRIENDS
 JUST PUT ME DOWN

Copyright Control

THE LEADER

ATOM SECRETS, SECRET LEAFLET, HAVE THE BOYS FOUND THE LEAK YET? THE MOLEHILL SETS THE WHEEL IN MOTION, HIS DOWNFALL PICKS UP LOCOMOTION.....

THE LEADERS WIFE TAKES A GOVERNMENT CAR
IN THE DARK TO MEET HER MINISTER
BUT THE LEADER NEVER LEAVES HIS DOOR AJAR
AS HE SWINGS HIS WHIP FROM THE BOER WAR...

HE WORE A LEATHER MASK FOR HIS DINNER GUESTS
TOTALLY NUDE AND WITH DEEP RESPECT
HE PROPOSED A TOAST TO THE VOTES HE GETS
 THE FEELING OF POWER, AND THE 'THOUGHT OF SEX!'

THE GIRL LET THE FAT MAN TOUCH HER
VODKA FUMES AND THE FEEL OF A VULTURE
THE DRIVER WAITED IN THE EMBASSY CAR
THE FAT MANS TRAP WAS SET FOR CAPTURE...
SO THE GIRL, LET THE THIN MAN TOUCH HER
MIXING QUESTIONS, DRUNKEN LAUGHTER
THE MINISTRY CAR WAS WAITING THERE
 A MINISTER KNOWS HIS OWN AFFAIR...

WELL THE PEOPLE MUST HAVE SOMETHING GOOD TO READ ON A SUNDAY

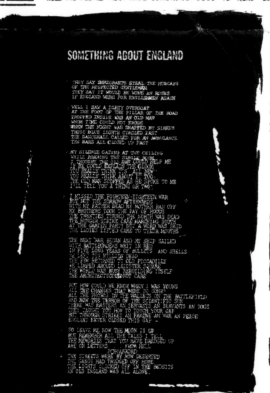

SOMETHING ABOUT ENGLAND

THEY SAY IMMIGRANTS STEAL THE HUBCAPS
OF THE RESPECTED GENTLEMEN
THEY SAY IT WOULD BE WINE AND ROSES
IF ENGLAND WERE FOR ENGLISHMEN AGAIN

WELL I SAW A DIRTY OVERCOAT
AT THE FOOT OF THE PILLAR OF THE ROAD
PROPPED INSIDE WAS AN OLD MAN
WHOM TIME COULD NOT EROD
WHEN THE NIGHT WAS SNAPPED BY SIRENS
THOSE BLUE LIGHTS CIRCLED FAST
THE DANCEHALL CALLED FOR AN AMBULANCE
THE BARS ALL CLOSED UP FAST

MY SILENCE GAZING AT THE CEILING
WHILE BREAKING THE OLD MAN'S BREAD
I THOUGHT HE COULD HELP ME
OR HE COULD EXPLAIN THE ODDS
YOU REALLY THINK ABOUT IN POD,
THE OLD MAN SCOFFED AS HE SPOKE TO ME
I'LL TELL YOU A THING OR TWO

I MISSED THE FOURTEEN-EIGHTEEN WAR
BUT NOT THE SORROW AFTERWARDS
WITH MY FATHER DEAD BY NOTHER RAN OFF
MY BROTHERS TOOK THE FAY OF HOODS
THE TWENTIES TURNED THE NORTH WAS DEAD
THE HUNGER TIPPED OUR CARE MARCHING SOUTH
AT THE CARDIFF PARTY WAS NO MORE SAID
THE LADIES LIFTED CAKES TO THEIR MOUTHS

THE NEXT WAR BEGAN AND MY SHIP SAILED
WITH BATTLE ORDERS WRIT IN RED
IN FIVE LONG YEARS OF BULLETS AND SHELLS
WE CAME BACK - OUR MATES WERE DEAD
THE JEW SENTENCE OF OLD PICCADILLY
WAS LIMPED AROUND LEICESTER SQUARE
THE WORLD WAS BUSY REBUILDING ITSELF
THE ARCHITECT COMMAND CARE

BUT HOW COULD WE KNOW WHEN I WAS YOUNG
ALL THE CHANGES THAT WERE TO COME?
ALL THE DAYS LEFT IN THE BALANCE OF THE BATTLEFIELD
AND NOW THE TERROR OF THE SCIENTIFIC SUN
THERE WAS MASTERS AS SERVANTS AS SERVANTS AN DOGS
THEY TAUGHT ME HOW TO TOUCH YOUR CAP
BUT THROUGH STRIKE AN FAMINE AN WAR AN PEACE
ENGLAND NEVER CLOSED THIS GAP

SO LEAVE ME NOW THE MOON IS UP
BUT REMEMBER ALL THE TALES I TELL
THE MEMORIES THAT YOU HAVE DREDGED UP
ARE ON LETTERS FROM HELL
 FORWARDED
THE STREETS WERE BY NOW DESERVED
THE GANGS HAD TRUDGED OFF HOME
THE LIGHTS CLICKED OFF IN THE BEDSITS
AN OLD ENGLAND WAS ALL ALONE.

IVAN MEETS G.I. JOE

[4] DR PEPPER/THE CLASH

Recorded live at Dr Pepper
Music Festival, Pier 84, New
Jersey, September 2nd
1982/apart from songs on Disc
Two, which are marked.

SOUND: **5**

(DISC ONE)

1977 (INSTRUMENTAL ONLY)
THE LEADER (TAKES 1/2 AND 3)
RADIO CLASH
(WHICH RUNS INTO LONG JAM SESSION)
(ALL THE ABOVE WAS THE SOUNDCHECK)
LONDON CALLING
ONE MORE TIME
CAR JAMMING
KNOW YOUR RIGHTS
GUNS OF BRIXTON
STAY FREE
ROCK THE CASBAH
CAREER OPPORTUNITIES
THE MAGNIFICENT SEVEN
POLICE ON MY BACK
THE LEADER
JANIE JONES
RADIO CLASH
ENGLISH CIVIL WAR
SOMEBODY GOT MURDERED
CLAMPDOWN
I FOUGHT THE LAW

(DISC TWO)

I FOUGHT THE LAW
CHARLIE DON'T SURF
SHOULD I STAY OR SHOULD I GO
COMPLETE CONTROL
STRAIGHT TO HELL
BRAND NEW CADILLAC
WHITE MAN IN HAMMERSMITH PALAIS
WHITE RIOT
SIX SECONDS TO WATCH/
PLAYED BEFORE THE CLASH SHOW
CAPITOL AIR/
PLAYED AT BONDS NYC JUNE 1981
ALL THE YOUNG PUNKS/DEMO
THE JUMPING MASTER/MIKEY
DREAD
WHITE MAN IN HAMMERSMITH
PALAIS/DEMO
LOVE KILLS/INSTRUMENTAL
STRAIGHT SHOOTER/JOE STRUMMER
LONDON'S BURNING/BLUE KILLA

[5] AMERICAN TOUR MAY 1984

RECORDED AT THE PARAMOUNT THEATER, SEATTLE, WASHINGTON

ARE YOU RED.. Y
COMPLETE CONTROL
IN THE POURING RAIN
CLAMPDOWN

RECORDED AT THE UNIVERSITY OF OREGON, EUGENE

SEX MAD ROAR
JANIE JONES
STRAIGHT TO HELL

RECORDED AT ARAGON BALLROOM, CHICAGO

CLASH CITY ROCKERS
THREE CARD TRICK
SAFE EUROPEAN HOME
WHITE RIOT

SOUND: **7**

[6] RUDE BOY/SOUNDTRACK

ENGLISH CIVIL WAR
WHITE MAN IN HAMMERSMITH
I'M SO BORED WITH THE USA
JANIE JONES
WHITE RIOT
COMPLETE CONTROL
TOMMY GUN
I FOUGHT THE LAW

SAFE EUROPEAN HOME
WHAT'S MY NAME?
POLICE & THIEVES
LONDON'S BURNING
WHITE RIOT
LET THE GOOD TIMES ROLL
GARAGELAND

SOUND: **7**

Above: The Right Profile x 3.
Below: Promo postcard for The Essential Clash compilation.

THE Essential CLASH

INCLUDES: London Calling
Rock The Casbah
Should I Stay or Should I Go
White Riot
I Fought The Law
Police and Thieves
(White Man) in Hammersmith Palais
Bankrobber

41 TRACKS ON 2CDs

IT'S A COMMON THING TO HEAR FROM CLASH
FANS THAT "THE GROUP CHANGED MY LIFE".
AND HOW MANY BANDS CAN CLAIM THAT?

OUT NOW
COLUMBIA
www.sonymusic.co.uk/theclash

COMING SOON...THE Essential CLASH DVD

(7) DIRTY HARRY

(RUNNING TIME: 44 MINUTES 22 SECONDS)

DIRTY HARRY/ORIGINAL MIX OF
'MAGNIFICENT SEVEN' BY MICK JONES
FINGERPOPPIN'/AOR MIX
1977/PROMO VIDEO VERSION
WHITE RIOT/PROMO VIDEO VERSION
LONDON'S BURNING/PROMO VIDEO
VERSION
RUDE BOY/MOVIE TRAILER
ARMAGIDEON TIME/LIVE FROM
CONCERT FOR KAMPUCHEA
STRAIGHT TO HELL/LIVE FROM
SATURDAY NIGHT LIVE
SHOULD I STAY OR SHOULD I
GO/LIVE FROM SATURDAY NIGHT LIVE

COOL CONFUSION/
ALTERNATIVE VERSION
THIS IS ENGLAND/DUTCH PROMO
SINGLE VERSION
VACKER VARLD/
IT'S A BEAUTIFUL WORLD
ONCE A PUNK ALWAYS A
PUNK/TOPPER HEADON
U.S. NOW/
RECORDED LIVE ON MARCH 4TH 1987
BY B.A.D. AT THE ASTORIA LONDON

SOUND: **8**

(8) RECORDED LIVE AT THE APOLLO THEATRE, MANCHESTER, FEBRUARY 3RD, 1980

(RUNNING TIME: 76 MINUTES 36 SECONDS)

RECORDED LIVE AT THE APOLLO
THEATER, MANCHESTER, ENGLAND,
FEBRUARY 3, 1980

CLASH CITY ROCKERS
BRAND NEW CADILLAC
SAFE EUROPEAN HOME
JIMMY JAZZ
LONDON CALLING
GUNS OF BRIXTON
PROTEX BLUE
TRAIN IN VAIN
KOKA KOLA
I FOUGHT THE LAW
WHITE MAN IN HAMMERSMITH
BANKROBBER
THE CLAMPDOWN

WRONG 'EM BOYO
STAY FREE
POLICE & THIEVES
CAPITOL RADIO
JANIE JONES
COMPLETE CONTROL
ARMAGIDEON TIME
ENGLISH CIVIL WAR
GARAGELAND
(DURING WHICH THE TAPE JUST STOPS!!)

SOUND: **6**

(9) LIVE AT THE LYCEUM BALLROOM, LONDON, OCTOBER 21ST, 1981

(RUNNING TIME DISC ONE: 69 MINUTES 40 SECONDS)
(RUNNING TIME DISC TWO: 41 MINUTES 26 SECONDS)

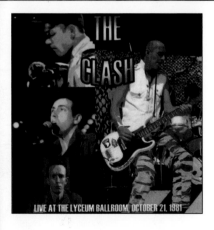

LIVE AT THE LYCEUM BALLROOM, OCTOBER 21, 1981

(DISC ONE)
BROADWAY
ONE MORE TIME
KNOW YOUR RIGHTS
GUNS OF BRIXTON
TRAIN IN VAIN
WHITE MAN IN HAMMERSMITH
THE MAGNIFICENT SEVEN
WRONG 'EM BOYO
CLASH CITY ROCKERS
KOKA KOLA
IVAN MEETS GI JOE
JUNCO PARTNER
THE LEADER
I FOUGHT THE LAW
CHARLIE DON'T SURF
SOMEBODY GOT MURDERED
LONDON CALLING
CLAMPDOWN
THIS IS RADIO CLASH

(DISC TWO)
CAREER OPPORTUNITIES
ARMAGIDEON TIME
JULIE'S BEEN WORKING FOR THE
DRUG SQUAD
STAY FREE
SAFE EUROPEAN HOME
POLICE & THIEVES
SHOULD I STAY OR SHOULD I GO
GRAFFITI RAP
JANIE JONES
BRAND NEW CADILLAC
LONDON'S BURNING
COMPLETE CONTROL

SOUND: **10**

(10) THE CLASH IN CONCERT, BONDS INTERNATIONAL CASINO, NEW YORK

(RUNNING TIME DISC ONE: 56 MINUTES 27 SECONDS)
(RUNNING TIME DISC TWO: 55 MINUTES 12 SECONDS)

(DISC ONE)
LONDON CALLING
SAFE EUROPEAN HOME
THE LEADER
TRAIN IN VAIN
WHITE MAN IN HAMMERSMITH
THIS IS RADIO CLASH
CORNER SOUL
THE GUNS OF BRIXTON
THE CALL UP
BANKROBBER
COMPLETE CONTROL
LIGHTNING STRIKES
IVAN MEETS GI JOE

(DISC TWO)
CHARLIE DON'T SURF
THE MAGNIFICENT SEVEN
BROADWAY
SOMEBODY GOT MURDERED
POLICE & THIEVES
THE CLAMPDOWN
ONE MORE TIME
BRAND NEW CADILLAC
THE STREET PARADE
JANIE JONES
WASHINGTON BULLETS

SOUND: 9

(11) NO ELVIS, BEATLES OR THE ROLLING STONES...

(RUNNING TIME DISC ONE: 71 MINUTES 46 SECONDS)
(RUNNING TIME DISC TWO: 72 MINUTES 50 SECONDS)

(DISC ONE)
LONDON CALLING
WHITE MAN IN HAMMERSMITH
WHAT'S MY NAME
SOMEBODY GOT MURDERED
POLICE & THIEVES
JAIL GUITAR DOORS
LOST IN A SUPERMARKET
CLASH CITY ROCKERS
BRAND NEW CADILLAC
JIMMY JAZZ
I'M SO BORED OF THE USA
COMPLETE CONTROL
THE MAGNIFICENT SEVEN
STRAIGHT TO HELL
CAPITOL RADIO
GUNS ON THE ROOF
SAFE EUROPEAN HOME
POLICE ON MY BACK
STAY FREE
BANKROBBER
GARAGELAND
JOE DISCUSSES BOOTLEGS

(DISC TWO)
CLAMPDOWN
DEATH OR GLORY
LONDON'S BURNING
KNOW YOUR RIGHTS
KOKA KOLA
ARMAGIDEON TIME
I FOUGHT THE LAW
DENY
SPANISH BOMBS
CAREER OPPORTUNITIES
TOMMY GUN
THE LEADER
TRAIN IN VAIN
WHITE RIOT
1977
THIS IS RADIO CLASH
SHOULD I STAY OR SHOULD I GO
WRONG 'EM BOYO
HATE & WAR
DRUGSTABBING TIME
JANIE JONES
ROCK THE CASBAH
CITY OF THE DEAD
JOE & MICK ON THE CLASH'S
LEGACY

SOUND: 6

BOOT

[12] STRIKING MINERS BENEFIT SHOW

(RUNNING TIME DISC ONE: 67 MINUTES 5 SECONDS)
(RUNNING TIME DISC TWO: 16 MINUTES 22 SECONDS)

(DISC ONE)
ONE MORE TIME
LONDON'S BURNING
COMPLETE CONTROL
THIS IS RADIO CLASH
SPANISH BOMBS
ROCK THE CASBAH
NORTH & SOUTH
ARE YOU READY FOR WAR?
WHAT'S MY NAME
THE DICTATOR
CAPITOL RADIO
BROADWAY
TOMMY GUN

BRAND NEW CADILLAC
WE ARE THE CLASH
ARMAGIDEON TIME
CAREER OPPORTUNITIES
BANKROBBER
THREE CARD TRICK
GARAGELAND

(DISC TWO)
DIRTY PUNK
AMMUNITION
WHITE RIOT
SAFE EUROPEAN HOME
LONDON CALLING

SOUND: 7

[13] SHIBOYA KOHKAIDO, TOKYO

(RUNNING TIME DISC ONE: 63 MINUTES 29 SECONDS)
(RUNNING TIME DISC TWO: 26 MINUTES 32 SECONDS)

(DISC ONE)
INTRO
SHOULD I STAY OR SHOULD I GO
ONE MORE TIME
SAFE EUROPEAN HOME
KNOW YOUR RIGHTS
TRAIN IN VAIN
WHITE MAN IN HAMMERSMITH
MAGNIFICENT SEVEN
GUNS OF BRIXTON
CHARLIE DON'T SURF
THE LEADER
IVAN MEETS GI JOE
JUNCO PARTNER
BROADWAY
STAY FREE
LONDON CALLING

(DISC TWO)
JANIE JONES
SOMEBODY GOT MURDERED
CLAMPDOWN
THIS IS RADIO CLASH
BRAND NEW CADILLAC
ARMAGIDEON TIME
LONDON'S BURNING

SOUND: 6

LEGS

Above: The not so Lone Rangers: Simonon and Strummer.
Below: Combat Rock era Clash.

Paul Simonon 1978 Photo: Sheila Rock/Rex Features

LYCEUM BALLROOM
Box office open 12-6 Mon-Sat.
8 pm. (normal sessions)
Telephone : 036 3715

SUNDAY
OCTOBER **25**

at 7.30 p.m.

Straight Music presents
The CLASH

№ 413

This portion to be retained
(P.T.O.)

LYCEUM BALLROOM
Box office open 12-6 Mon-Sat.
8 pm. (normal sessions)
Telephone : 036 3715

MONDAY
OCTOBER **26**

at 7.30 p.m.

Straight Music presents
The CLASH

№ 1911

This portion to be retained
(P.T.O.)

[14] "THIS IS THE HOUSE OF THE BLUES, RIGHT?"

(RUNNING TIME: 46 MINUTES 23 SECONDS)

AIN'T GOT NO REASON
LET THE GOOD TIMES ROLL
(BOTH TAKEN FROM THE FILM
'RUDE BOY')
JIMMY JAZZ
I'M SO BORED OF THE USA
COMPLETE CONTROL
LONDON CALLING
CLAMPDOWN
WHITE MAN IN HAMMERSMITH
KOKA KOLA
I FOUGHT THE LAW
JAIL GUITAR DOORS
POLICE & THIEVES

STAY FREE
CLASH CITY ROCKERS
SAFE EUROPEAN HOME
CAPITOL RADIO ONE
JANIE JONES
GARAGELAND
JUSTICE TONIGHT/KICK IT OVER
CAREER OPPORTUNITIES
WHITE RIOT

SOUND: 8

[15] US FESTIVAL WARM-UP CONCERT

(RUNNING TIME DISC ONE: 47 MINUTES 17 SECONDS)
(RUNNING TIME DISC TWO: 64 MINUTES 6 SECONDS)

SOUND: 7

(DISC ONE)

GARAGELAND
SPANISH BOMBS
SOMEBODY GOT MURDERED
ARMAGIDEON TIME
ROCK THE CASBAH
LOST IN A SUPERMARKET
KNOW YOUR RIGHTS
CHARLIE DON'T SURF
GUNS OF BRIXTON
I'M SO BORED OF THE USA
DEATH OR GLORY
BANKROBBER

(DISC TWO)

HATE & WAR
TOMMY GUN
SOUND OF THE SINNERS
POLICE ON MY BACK
BRAND NEW CADILLAC
LONDON CALLING
STRAIGHT TO HELL
TRAIN IN VAIN
THE MAGNIFICENT SEVEN
FINGERNAILS
SHOULD I STAY OR SHOULD I GO

[16] ALRIGHT NOW

(RUNNING TIME: 8 MINUTES 38 SECONDS)

RARELY DO YOU EVER FIND BOOTLEG SINGLES OR EP'S, BUT THIS MAY BE THE EXCEPTION...

ENGLISH CIVIL WAR
INTERVIEW
HATE & WAR
THE ISRAELITES AKA 'ME EARS
ARE ALIGHT!'

SOUND: 10

[17] THE GUNS OF BRIXTON

(RUNNING TIME: 77 MINUTES 35 SECONDS)

SAFE EUROPEAN HOME
I'M SO BORED WITH THE USA
COMPLETE CONTROL
LONDON CALLING
WHITE MAN IN HAMMERSMITH
KOKA KOLA
I FOUGHT THE LAW
JAIL GUITAR DOORS
THE GUNS OF BRIXTON
ENGLISH CIVIL WAR
CLASH CITY ROCKERS
STAY FREE
CLAMPDOWN
POLICE & THIEVES

CAPITOL RADIO ONE
TOMMY GUN
WRONG 'EM BOYO
JANIE JONES
GARAGELAND
ARMAGIDEON TIME
CAREER OPPORTUNITIES
WHAT'S MY NAME
WHITE RIOT

SOUND: 7

[18] RECORDED LIVE AT LIVERPOOL ROYAL COURT

(RUNNING TIME DISC ONE: 65 MINUTES 5 SECONDS)
(RUNNING TIME DISC TWO: 35 MINUTES 4 SECONDS)

Recorded on March 5th 1984.

[DISC ONE]
LONDON CALLING
SAFE EUROPEAN HOME
BAND INTROS
ARE YOU READY FOR WAR?
SEX MAD ROAR
KNOW YOUR RIGHTS
GUNS OF BRIXTON
AMMUNITION
THE CLAMPDOWN
RADIO CLASH
CLASH CITY ROCKERS
THIS IS ENGLAND
I'M SO BORED WITH THE USA
CAREER OPPORTUNITIES
WHITE MAN IN HAMMERSMITH

POLICE & THIEVES
THREE CARD TRICK
JANIE JONES
I FOUGHT THE LAW

[DISC TWO]
TOMMY GUN
REMOTE CONTROL
ENGLISH CIVIL WAR
BRAND NEW CADILLAC
ARMAGIDEON TIME
SHOULD I STAY OR SHOULD I GO?
GARAGELAND
BANK ROBBER
SPANISH BOMBS
WHITE RIOT

SOUND: 5

[19] ACOUSTIC DAZE

(RUNNING TIME: 47 MINUTES 45 SECONDS)

MOVERS & SHAKERS
COOL UNDER HEAT
GUNS OF BRIXTON
SPANISH BOMBS
POLICE ON MY BACK
JIMMY JAZZ
WHITE MAN IN HAMMERSMITH
STRAIGHT TO HELL
CLASH CITY ROCKERS
I FOUGHT THE LAW
BRAND NEW CADILLAC
WHITE RIOT

BANKROBBER
STEPPING STONE

SOUND: 7

(20) ELVIS HAS LEFT THE BUILDING...

(RUNNING TIME: 29 MINUTES 47 SECONDS)

KING OF ROCK N' ROLL
BLONDIE ROCK N' ROLL
WHITE RIOT (REHEARSAL VERSION)
KNOW YOUR RIGHTS (ALTERNATIVE
TAKE)
1977 (REHEARSAL VERSION)
OVERPOWERED BY FUNK
(INSTRUMENTAL)
LOUIE LOUIE
GARAGELAND (RUDE BOY COMPLETE
OUTTAKE)
HOUSE OF THE JU JU QUEEN
(DEMO VERSION)
YMCA (WCBN RADIO VERSION)

SOUND: **8**

(21) IF MUSIC COULD TALK...

(RUNNING TIME: 63 MINUTES 29 SECONDS)

PAUL
JUNCO PARTNER
PAUL
ONE MORE TIME
PAUL
MICK
HITSVILLE UK
MICK
THE MAGNIFICENT SEVEN
JOE
WASHINGTON BULLETS
JOE
THE CALL UP
JOE

POLICE ON MY BACK
TOPPER
IVAN MEETS GI JOE
TOPPER
SOMEBODY GOT MURDERED

BONUS TRACKS FROM
INTERCHORDS:

MICK
JOE
PAUL
PAUL
PAUL

SOUND: **10**

(22) GIVE 'EM ENOUGH DOPE

(RUNNING TIME: 62 MINUTES 27 SECONDS)

TRAIN IN VAIN
WASHINGTON BULLETS
IVAN MEETS GI JOE
CAREER OPPORTUNITIES
JANIE JONES
CLASH CITY ROCKERS
LONDON'S BURNING
(RECORDED AT THE SUN PLAZA
TOKYO FEBRUARY IST 1982)
ARE YOU READY FOR WAR?
COMPLETE CONTROL
IN THE POURING RAIN

CLAMPDOWN
THE SEX MAD ROAR
JANIE JONES
STRAIGHT TO HELL
BRAND NEW CADILLAC
CLASH CITY ROCKERS
THREE CARD TRICK
SAFE EUROPEAN HOME
WHITE RIOT
(RECORDED LIVE IN THE USA MAY
1984, WITH THE CLASH MARK 2
LINE-UP)

SOUND: **8**

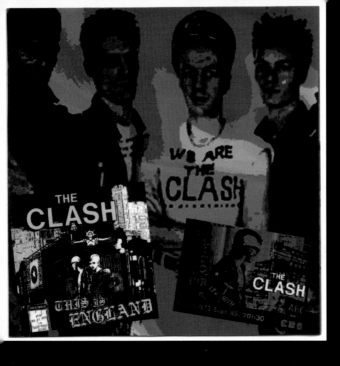

"I THINK THEY ARE THE FIRST BAND TO COME ALONG WHO'LL REALLY FRIGHTEN THE SEX PISTOLS SHITLESS."
(GIOVANNI DADOMO)

(23) WHO'S ON FIRST ?
(RUNNING TIME: 51 MINUTES 6 SECONDS)

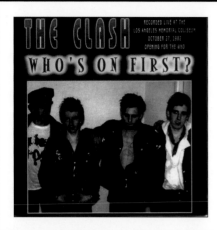

Recorded live at The Los Angeles Memorial Coliseum, October 27th 1982.
(While Supporting The Who).

LONDON CALLING
POLICE ON MY BACK
THE GUNS OF BRIXTON
THIS IS RADIO CLASH
SPANISH BOMBS
ROCK THE CASBAH
THE MAGNIFICENT SEVEN
ARMAGIDEON TIME
THE MAGNIFICENT SEVEN/REPRISE
JANIE JONES

TRAIN IN VAIN
TOMMY GUN
THE CLAMPDOWN
BRAND NEW CADILLAC
SHOULD I STAY OR SHOULD I GO?
I FOUGHT THE LAW

SOUND: 6

(24) COMBAT ROCK/THE ORIGINAL MICK JONES MIXES
(RUNNING TIME: 67 MINUTES 59 SECONDS)

KNOW YOUR RIGHTS
CAR JAMMING
ROCK THE CASBAH
RED ANGEL DRAGNET
SHOULD I STAY OR SHOULD I GO
GHETTO DEFENDANT
STRAIGHT TO HELL
INNOCULATED CITY
ATOM TAN
COOL CONFUSION
SEAN FLYNN

DEATH IS A STAR
FIRST NIGHT BACK IN LONDON
THE BEAUTIFUL PEOPLE ARE UGLY
TOO
KILL TIME

SOUND: 6

(25) LIVE AT THE TRIBAL STOMP FESTIVAL, MONTEREY, CALIFORNIA, 09/08/1979
(RUNNING TIME: 56 MINUTES 58 SECONDS)

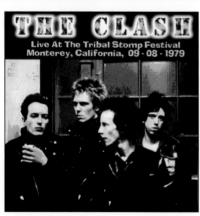

I'M SO BORED WITH THE USA
COMPLETE CONTROL
LONDON CALLING
JAIL GUITAR DOORS
WHITE MAN IN HAMMERSMITH
DRUG STABBING TIME
POLICE & THIEVES
STAY FREE
CAPITOL RADIO
CLASH CITY ROCKERS
WHAT'S MY NAME?
JANIE JONES

GARAGELAND
ARMAGIDEON TIME
CAREER OPPORTUNITIES
I KEEP MY FINGERNAILS LONG
(WITH JOE ELY)
WHITE RIOT

SOUND: 9

(26) SUPER GOLDEN RADIO SHOWS NO. 28/ THE CLASH LIVE IN CARDIFF 1977

(RUNNING TIME: 34 MINUTES 29 SECONDS)

I'M SO BORED WITH THE USA
HATE & WAR
48 HOURS
DENY
POLICE & THIEVES
CHEAT
CAPITOL RADIO ONE
WHAT'S MY NAME
PROTEX BLUE
REMOTE CONTROL
GARAGELAND
1977

SOUND: 6

(27) THE CLASH INTO THE 80'S

(RUNNING TIME: 66 MINUTES 15 SECONDS)

Recorded at The Lochern
Festival 20th May 1982.

LONDON CALLING
SAFE EUROPEAN HOME
GUNS OF BRIXTON
TRAIN IN VAIN
CLASH CITY ROCKERS
KNOW YOUR RIGHTS
MAGNIFICENT SEVEN
GHETTO DEFENDANT
SHOULD I STAY OR SHOULD I GO
POLICE & THIEVES
BRAND NEW CADILLAC
BANKROBBER
COMPLETE CONTROL
CAREER OPPORTUNITIES
CLAMPDOWN

SOUND: 7

(28) DEMOS 1976 - 1979

(RUNNING TIME: 62 MINUTES 25 SECONDS)

SOUND: 9

CAREER OPPORTUNITIES
WHITE RIOT
JANIE JONES
LONDON'S BURNING
1977
(RECORDED AT POLYDOR STUDIOS
DECEMBER 1976)
1-2 CRUSH ON YOU
PRESSURE DROP
THE PRISONER
(RECORDED AT CBS STUDIOS
JANUARY 1978)
SAFE EUROPEAN HOME
JULIE'S BEEN WORKING FOR THE
DRUG SQUAD

GROOVY TIMES
DRUG STABBING TIME
LAST GANG IN TOWN
OOH BABY OOH
ONE EMOTION
(GIVE 'EM ENOUGH ROPE DEMOS
AND OUTTAKES 1978)
YOU CAN'T JUDGE A WOMAN/BY
MAKING LOVE TO HER MOTHER
(RECORDED AT WESSEX STUDIOS
1979)
KILL TIME!
(RECORDED IN NEW YORK LIVE
APRIL 1982)

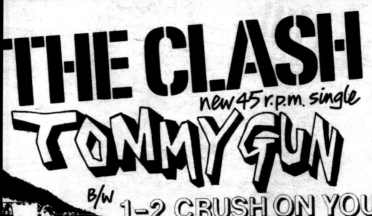

THE CLASH
new 45 r.p.m. single
TOMMY GUN
B/W
1-2 CRUSH ON YOU
(previously unavailable)

THE CLASH
'SORT IT OUT TOUR' CONTINUES
December 2 Polytechnic, Newcastle
12 Pavilion, Bath

THE NEW SINGLE BY THE CLASH

REMOTE CONTROL

and LONDON'S BURNING - LIVE

CBS 5293

CBS

The Clash

VINYL STICKER

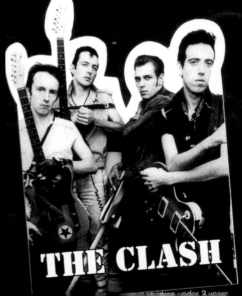

THE CLASH

I'M SO BORED WITH THE USA
HATE & WAR
48 HOURS
DENY
POLICE & THIEVES
CHEAT
CAPITOL RADIO
WHAT'S MY NAME
PROTEX BLUE
REMOTE CONTROL
GARAGELAND
1977
CLASH CITY ROCKERS
TOMMY GUN
(LIVE ON UK TELEVISION FEB 1978)
WHITE RIOT
(LIVE AT ANL FESTIVAL 30TH APRIL 1978)

THE BEAUTIFUL PEOPLE ARE UGLY TOO
(COMBAT ROCK OUT TAKE 1982)
LISTEN
CAPITOL RADIO
INTERVIEW WITH TONY PARSONS
(THE NME FREEBIE)
MONA
(RECORDED LIVE IN AUGUST 1979)
SHOULD I STAY OR SHOULD I GO
TRAIN IN VAIN
(UNDATED LIVE VERSIONS)
THE KEYS TO YOUR HEART
(101'ERS DEBUT SINGLE/JOE
STRUMMER'S FIRST BAND)

SOUND: 6

Main gig recorded live at The Roundhouse Camden, featuring a five-man Clash with Keith Levene on guitar, September 5th 1976.

DENY
1-2 CRUSH ON YOU
I KNOW WHAT TO DO
I DON'T WANT YOUR MONEY
I CAN'T UNDERSTAND THE FILES
PROTEX BLUE
JANIE JONES
MARK ME ABSENT
GOING TO THE DISCO
48 HOURS
I'M SO BORED WITH YOU
WORK
LONDON'S BURNING
WHAT'S MY NAME?
1977

WHITE RIOT
BIRMINGHAM'S BURNING
I'M SO BORED WITH THE USA
I CAN'T UNDERSTAND THE FILES
PROTEX BLUE
GOING TO THE DISCO
DENY
CAREER OPPORTUNITIES
48 HOURS
WHAT'S MY NAME
JANIE JONES
1977
1-2 CRUSH ON YOU
(RECORDED AT BARBARELLAS
BIRMINGHAM 26TH
OCTOBER 1976)

SOUND: 7

LONDON CALLING
SAFE EUROPEAN HOME
THE LEADER
TRAIN IN VAIN
THIS IS RADIO CLASH
GUNS OF BRIXTON
THE CALL UP
BANKROBBER
CHARLIE DON'T SURF
THE MAGNIFICENT SEVEN
(RECORDED LIVE AT PIER 57 NEW
YORK CITY NOVEMBER 1981)
MONA

UNTITLED/REGGAE RULES
IT'S NOT OVER
MYSTERY SONG
CAN'T JUDGE A BOOK BY LOOKIN'
AT THE COVER
(UNRELEASED DEMOS 1977 - 1980)
MAGNIFICENT SEVEN
(THE TOM SYNDER SHOW 1980)
WASHINGTON BULLETS
IVAN MEETS GI JOE
CAREER OPPORTUNITIES
JANIE JONES
(RECORDED LIVE IN TOKYO FEB 1982)

SOUND: 7

Last Gang In Town (original cover) Combat Rock — Epic records promo book (front & back covers)

(32) CLASH CALLING (RUNNING TIME: 69 MINUTES 12 SECONDS)

LONDON CALLING
SOMEBODY GOT MURDERED
ROCK THE CASBAH
GUNS OF BRIXTON
THESE ARE YOUR RIGHTS
KOKA KOLA
HATE OR WAR
ARMAGIDEON TIME
AIN'T GOOD ENOUGH
SAFE EUROPEAN HOME
POLICE ON MY BACK
BRAND NEW CADILLAC
I FOUGHT THE LAW
I'M SO BORED WITH THE USA
STAND BY ME

MAGNIFICENT SEVEN
STRAIGHT TO HELL
SHOULD I STAY OR SHOULD I GO
CLAMPDOWN

SOUND: 7

(33) YELLOW RIOT (RUNNING TIME: 53 MINUTES 3 SECONDS)

LONDON CALLING
SAFE EUROPEAN HOME
WHITE MAN IN HAMMERSMITH
BRAND NEW CADILLAC
CHARLIE DON'T SURF
CLAMPDOWN

THIS IS RADIO CLASH
ARMAGIDEON TIMES
JIMMY JAZZ
TOMMY GUN
POLICE ON MY BACK
WHITE RIOT

Recorded live in Japan during 1978

SOUND: 8

(34) FRANCE 1981 (RUNNING TIME: 73 MINUTES 30 SECONDS)

LONDON CALLING
SAFE EUROPEAN HOME
THE LEADER
SOMEBODY GOT MURDERED
WHITE MAN IN HAMMERSMITH
GUN OF BRIXTON
LIGHTENING STRIKES
I FOUGHT THE LAW

CORNER SOUL
IVAN MEETS GI JOE
RADIO CLASH
CHARLIE DON'T SURF
MAGNIFICENT SEVEN
BANKROBBER
WRONG 'EM BOYO
TRAIN IN VAIN

Recorded live at Palais St Sauveur on May 9th 1981.

SOUND: 6

(35) LOCHERN FESTIVAL

(RUNNING TIME: 68 MINUTES 43 SECONDS)

LONDON CALLING
SAFE EUROPEAN HOME
GUNS OF BRIXTON
TRAIN IN VAIN
CLASH CITY ROCKERS
KNOW YOUR RIGHTS
THE MAGNIFICENT SEVEN
GHETTO DEFENDANT
SHOULD I STAY OR SHOULD I GO
POLICE & THIEVES
BRAND NEW CADILLAC
BANKROBBER
COMPLETE CONTROL
CAREER OPPORTUNITIES
THE CLAMPDOWN
BONUS TRACKS:

RETURN TO BRIXTON (ALL MIXES)
BETTER SOUND THAN GIG.

SOUND: **5**

(36) JAMAICAN AFFAIR

(RUNNING TIME: 67 MINUTES 10 SECONDS)

LONDON CALLING
POLICE ON MY BACK
THE GUNS OF BRIXTON
THE MAGNIFICENT SEVEN
(INCLUDING ARMAGIDEON TIME JAM)
JUNCO PARTNER
SPANISH BOMB
ONE MORE TIME
TRAIN IN VAIN

BANKROBBER
THIS IS RADIO CLASH
CLAMPDOWN
SHOULD I STAY OR SHOULD I GO
ROCK THE CASBAH
STRAIGHT TO HELL
I FOUGHT THE LAW

Recorded in Kingston Jamaica 1982.

SOUND: **7**

(37) COMBAT OUT ROCK

(RUNNING TIME: 66 MINUTES 54 SECONDS)

KNOW YOUR RIGHTS
CAR JAMMING
ROCK THE CASBAH
RED ANGEL DRAGNET
SHOULD I STAY OR SHOULD I GO
GHETTO DEFENDANT
STRAIGHT TO HELL
INNOCULATED CITY

ATOM TAN
COOL CONFUSION
SEAN FLYNN
DEATH IS A STAR
FIRST NIGHT BACK IN LONDON
UNRELEASED AND UNTITLED SONGS
X 2

(THIS IS THE ORIGINAL MICK JONES MIX OF THE ALBUM THAT WAS
NEARLY CALLED RAT PATROL FROM FORT BRAGG)

SOUND: **7**

(38) STRUMMERVILLE

KEY'S TO YOUR HEART
(THE 101ERS)
TRASH CITY
LOVE KILLS
GANGSTERVILLE
(JOE STRUMMER)
I FOUGHT THE LAW
LONDON CALLING
(JOE STRUMMER & THE POGUES)
ISHEN
DIGGIN' THE NEW
BRAND NEW CADILLAC
WHITE MAN IN HAMMERSMITH PALAIS
TOMMY GUN
(JOE STRUMMER & THE

MESCALEROS)
IT'S A ROCKIN' WORLD
(FROM SOUTH PARK CHEF AID)
POURING RAIN
(THE CLASH 2)
ROCK THE CASBAH/DANCE MIX
THIS IS RADIO CLASH/LONG
VERSION
(THE CLASH)

SOUND: **7**

(39) SID VICIOUS & MICK JONES LIVE AT MAX'S

SEARCH AND DESTROY
I WANNA BE YOUR DOG
NO LIP
SOMETHING ELSE
BELSEN WAS A GAS
STEPPIN' STONE
CHINESE ROCKS
MY WAY

TAKE A CHANCE

A performance from July 9th 1978 at the famous New York club, this recording should not be confused with the official Virgin records album 'Sid Sings'.

SOUND: **6**

(40) CLASH ON BROADWAY 4

SOUND: **10**

ROCK THE CASBAH/WITH RANKIN RODGER
GUN OF BRIXTON/ALTERNATIVE MIX
TRAIN IN VAIN/REMIX
WHITE MAN IN
HAMMERSMITH/ALTERNATIVE RAR
GLUE ZOMBIE/GLASGOW 10TH
FEBRUARY 1984
THIS IS ENGLAND/ALTERNATIVE MIX
IN THE POURING RAIN/SEATTLE
30TH MAY 1984
ARE YOU READY FOR WAR/SEATTLE
30TH MAY 1984
FINGERPOPPIN/12" AOR MIX
BONDS REPORTS
DIRTY HARRY/FULL RADIO MIX
WE ARE THE CLASH

AMMUNITION/PARIS 1ST MAY 1984
UNKNOWN/COLUMBUS OHIO 9TH MAY
1984 (SOUNDCHECK)
KING OF THE ROAD/SANDINISTA
OUT-TAKE
BLONDE ROCK N' ROLL/ELLEN FOLEY
WHITE RIOT/APRIL 26TH 1977
PROMO VIDEO SHOOT
KNOW YOUR RIGHTS/COMBAT ROCK
OUT-TAKE
1977/APRIL 26TH 1977 PROMO
VIDEO SHOOT
OVERPOWERED BY FUNK/COMBAT
ROCK OUT-TAKE
LOUIE LOUIE/SANDINISTA OUT-TAKE
GARAGELAND/RUDE BOY OUT-TAKE
HOUSE OF THE JU JU QUEEN/DEMO
DECEMBER 1982
YMCA/WCBN RADIO SING-A-LONG

Made to look just like what might have been Disc 4 in the official 'Clash On Broadway' box set release. Even the disc is marked Promotional Only. I do advise you to find one. It's essential.

THE CLASH IN PRINT

Unlike some other bands of the same era (you'd be right to think of The Sex Pistols at this point) The Clash bookshelf is not exactly groaning under the weight of the books to be found on it. The band's musical and cultural significance is not reflected in print. At the time of writing, none of the band have an autobiography in print, although their road manager did an excellent job of his own book (which I'll come to in more detail later).

(1) THE CLASH SONIC BOOKS
WRITTEN BY VANNI NERI & GIORGIO CAMPANI.
(TEXT IN ENGLISH AND ITALIAN)

Found for a short time around 1998/1999 in some of the better import book shops (if you live in London, that would always be Helter Skelter, of whom more details later). This is a small CD size publication, which contains some very nice pictures (some that can only be found here). It also comes complete with a CD of Clash recordings, although the bootleg laws are totally different in Italy than they are in the UK. By any other name this is a bootleg CD – the disc itself featuring early demo recordings of the following songs:

CAREER OPPORTUNITIES
WHITE RIOT
JANIE JONES
LONDON'S BURNING
1977
LISTEN
1-2 CRUSH ON YOU

The running time on the disc is 17 minutes and 8 seconds, while the disc itself also carries the following code number: SIAE Sonic. 15.
I have seen the disc selling in a plain white card sleeve on its own at record fairs, but the book seems to have vanished as fast as it appeared.

(2) THE CLASH UNANIMOUS BOOKS
WRITTEN BY DAVID QUANTICK.

A breakdown of the group's story and recording studio details, written by former NME and current Q magazine scribe, it contains some very interesting details.

PAGES: 136
FORMAT: A5

THE CLASH

LIVE

Photo: Rex features

(3) THE CLASH RETROSPECTIVE RETRO PUBLISHING
WRITTEN BY AGENT PROVOCATEUR.

All the recorded releases to date by the group, including imports and very well illustrated in colour and black & white. I do know the Agent Provocateur personally, but telling you who he is would just spoil the fun.

PAGES: 120
FORMAT: A4

(4) THE CLASH BEFORE & AFTER
PLEXUS PUBLISHING
PHOTOS BY PENNIE SMITH.

A fantastic collection of Clash photos by the lady responsible for the London Calling sleeve. Classic black & white images and including passing comments from Mick, Joe, Paul and Topper.

(5) THE CLASH NEW VISUAL DOCUMENTARY OMNIBUS PRESS
WRITTEN BY MILES & JOHN TOBLER.

One of the first Clash books to see the light of day and still one of the best, dusted off and updated every once in a while. Very well informed.

PAGES: 116

FORMAT: A4

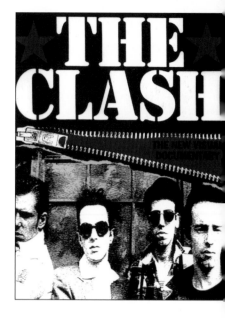

(6) A RIOT OF OUR OWN   INDIGO PUBLISHING
WRITTEN BY JOHNNY GREEN & GARRY BARKER (WITH A FOREWORD BY JOE STRUMMER).

This incredible book of on the road tales by The Clash's former tour manager had me laughing right through it. The book is illustrated by Ray Lowry with all new drawings. An absolute must for Clash fans.

(7) THE CLASH VIRGIN MODERN ICONS SERIES
WITH AN INTRODUCTION BY PAUL DU NOYER.

A collection of quotes from band members and friends, very well illustrated throughout in colour and black & white

PAGES: 94

FORMAT: A5

(8) THE CLASH: PHOTOGRAPHS BY BOB GRUEN
PUBLISHED BY VISION ON/PROUD GALLERIES.

Available in two formats, the first was hardback, which came in a cloth box and was a limited edition, while the second is paperback and still in the shops. A collection of perfect images by one of the greatest rock photographers ever to walk planet earth, you get the idea... Lavish.

(9) THE RETURN OF THE LAST GANG IN TOWN

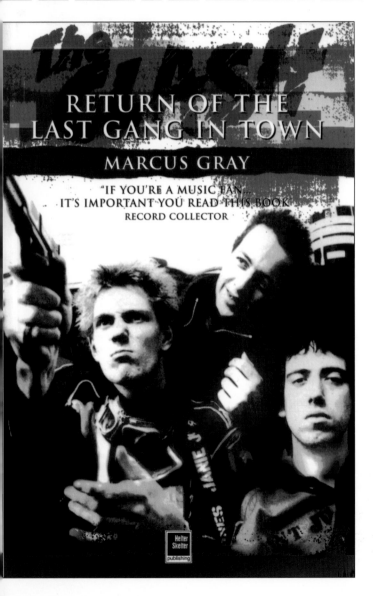

PUBLISHED BY HELTER SKELTER PUBLISHING
WRITTEN BY MARCUS GRAY.

Certainly the best Clash book to date, does for the group what Jon Savage's 'England's Dreaming' did for the Sex Pistols. Originally printed by Fourth Estate in 1995 under the title 'Last Gang In Town'.

IF YOU HAVE ANY PROBLEMS AT ALL OBTAINING BOOKS ON THE CLASH (OR ANY GROUP FOR THAT MATTER) CONTACT: HELTER SKELTER MUSIC BOOKSTORE, 4 DENMARK STREET, LONDON, WC2H 8LL

THEY CAN BE REACHED BY TELEPHONE ON: 44 (0) 207 836 1151.

THE CLASH HIGHEST UK CHART POSITIONS
(BASED ON UK TOP 40 ONLY)

Time now to solve all those 'down the pub' arguments regarding the records and where they charted...

(THE ALBUMS)

THE CLASH
Highest UK Chart Position: **12**

"The Clash album is like a mirror. It reflects all the shit. It shows the truth."
(Mark P, Sniffin' Glue)

GIVE 'EM ENOUGH ROPE
Highest UK Chart Position: **2**

"Ultimately, they'd make a debut album that would become arguably the most important punk record of them all."
(Sean Egan Uncut Magazine)

LONDON CALLING
Highest UK Chart Position: **9**

"The Clash love rock n' roll, which is why they play it, but they want to live up to its promises, which is why they play it the way they do. With groups like The Clash on the case, rock ain't in the cultural dumper: London Calling makes up for all the bad rock 'n' roll played over the last decade."
(Charles Shaar Murray, NME)

SANDINISTA!
Highest UK Chart Position: **19**

"The fourth Clash album is an adventure of diversity and wit, of struggle and freedom, of excellence..."
(Robbi Millar, Sounds)

COMBAT ROCK
Highest UK Chart Position: **2**

"Listen, I'll tell you where the 'socially concerned rock artist' stands in the bubblegum environment of today: s/he stands HERE!"
(X Moore, NME)

CUT THE CRAP
Highest UK Chart Position: **16**

"Even more than anything The Pistols ever did, The Clash's first album was to epitomise the punk stereotype. What were later to become cliches were, at the time, angry young innovations."
(NME)

TIME NOW TO SOLVE ALL THOSE 'DOWN THE PUB' ARGUMENTS... THE SEQUEL!

(THE SINGLES)

WHITE RIOT
Highest UK Chart Position: 38

"It's pointless to categorise this with other records: White Riot isn't a poxy single of the week, it's the first meaningful event all year."
(Tom Robinson, NME)

REMOTE CONTROL
Highest UK Chart Position: NEVER CHARTED

COMPLETE CONTROL
Highest UK Chart Position: 28

"Good though the Pistols' singles are, this knife-edged meisterwork makes mincemeat of them. Reggae and Punk are forever talked of in the same breath... now the relationship has been consummated."
(Ian Birch, Melody Maker)

CLASH CITY ROCKERS
Highest UK Chart Position: 35

(WHITE MAN) IN HAMMERSMITH PALAIS
Highest UK Position: 32

"Though this record contains the basic elements to turn the tables, as producers The Clash sell themselves far short of their obvious potential... There's absolutely nothing wrong with The Clash that a good producer couldn't rectify."   (Roy Carr, NME)

TOMMY GUN
Highest UK Chart Position: 19

ENGLISH CIVIL WAR
Highest UK Chart Position: 25

"The Clash do it monstrously well, cover their bases with such cunning, take upon themselves the lustre of an irresistible force..."
(Dave Hepworth, Sounds)

COST OF LIVING EP
Highest UK Chart Position: 22

LONDON CALLING
Highest UK Chart Position: 11

"An irresistibly rolling gait, finely underplayed performances and sweet harmonies on the title words. The lyrics are still apocalyptic clarion calls, but now Joe sings them with a natural assurance and clarity that make them much more forceful."   (Ian Birch,   Melody Maker)

BANKROBBER   Highest UK Chart Position: **12**

THE CALL UP   Highest UK Chart Position: **40**

HITSVILLE UK   Highest UK Chart Position: **NEVER CHARTED**

THE MAGNIFICENT SEVEN   Highest UK Chart Position: **34**

"A great record. It features a superb bassline, an intelligent lyric, and succeeds beautifully because Joe Strummer understands that the rhythm of his words are just as important as Mick Jones' funk guitar."
(Paolo Hewitt,   Melody Maker)

THIS IS RADIO CLASH   Highest UK Chart Position: **47**

"A sprawling, splintered fantasy which presents the zombified vision of would-be media guerrillas with rampant hysteria."
(Gavin Martin   NME)

KNOW YOUR RIGHTS   Highest UK Chart Position: **NEVER CHARTED**

ROCK THE CASBAH   Highest UK Chart Position: **30**

STRAIGHT TO HELL   Highest UK Chart Position: **17**

"Though it could well be the rambling Stonesy Should I Stay Or Should I Go that will pick up most of the airplay, it is Straight To Hell that is the reaffirmation that there is still life in The Clash."
(Adrian Thrills   NME)

THIS IS ENGLAND   Highest UK Chart Position: **16**

I FOUGHT THE LAW   Highest UK Chart Position: **29**

LONDON CALLING   Highest UK Chart Position: **NEVER CHARTED**

RETURN TO BRIXTON   Highest UK Chart Position: **NEVER CHARTED**

SHOULD I STAY OR SHOULD I GO   Highest UK Chart Position: **1**

(The last 4 singles were all released after the group had split)

"The Clash are coming... The Clash... The Clash... The Clash... In the late summer London of 1976 it wasn't easy to avoid those two words - snowflakes in a blizzard of fevered, word of mouth anticipation"
(Danny Kelly)

THE CLASH HIGHEST USA CHART POSITIONS

(THE ALBUMS)

THE CLASH   Highest USA Chart Position: **100**

"Better than other punk rock albums, The Clash convincingly vents its outrage and frustration... and backs them with simple, careful, driving rock."
(Charley Walters, Rolling Stone)

GIVE 'EM ENOUGH ROPE   Highest USA Chart Position: **128**

LONDON CALLING   Highest USA Chart Position: **27**

SANDINISTA!   Highest USA Chart Position: **24**

COMBAT ROCK   Highest USA Chart Position: **7**

CUT THE CRAP   Highest USA Chart Position: **85**

(THE SINGLES)

TOMMY GUN   Highest USA Chart Position: **NEVER CHARTED**

FOUGHT THE LAW   Highest USA Chart Position: **NEVER CHARTED**

TRAIN IN VAIN   Highest USA Chart Position: **27**

THE CALL UP   Highest USA Chart Position: **NEVER CHARTED**

HITSVILLE UK   Highest USA Chart Position: **NEVER CHARTED**

THIS IS RADIO CLASH   Highest USA Chart Position: **NEVER CHARTED**

KNOW YOUR RIGHTS   Highest USA Chart Position: **NEVER CHARTED**

ROCK THE CASBAH   Highest USA Chart Position: **8**

SHOULD I STAY OR SHOULD I GO   Highest USA Chart Position: **45**

THIS IS ENGLAND   Highest USA Chart Position: **88**

THE CLASH PRODUCERS

THE CLASH: MICKEY FOOTE (both UK & USA versions)

GIVE 'EM ENOUGH ROPE: SANDY PEARLMAN

LONDON CALLING: GUY STEVENS

SANDINISTA!:   JONES/STRUMMER/SIMONON/HEADON

COMBAT ROCK: GLYN JOHNS

CUT THE CRAP: STRUMMER WITH JOSE UNIDOS & BERNIE RHODES

The Clash.
Photographs by Bob Gruen.
Edited by Chris Salewicz.

✪ Including never before seen images and exclusive
interviews with the band. Published by Vision On,
luxury hardback with slipcase, price £45.

✪ Pre order your copy of The Clash and get a free
limited edition print, signed by Bob Gruen.

✪ To claim your print, simply place a customer order
for The Clash with your local bookshop.

✪ Send your postcard with your mailing address to
the following address, attaching your receipt as
proof of purchase:

Diana Bell (ref: The Clash)
Vision On, 112-116 Old Street
London, EC1V 9BG.

✪ The Clash, ISBN 1903399335.
✪ Distributed by Omnibus Press/Book Sales Ltd.
✪ For trade orders please call:

✪ Publication date: 17th September 2001.

Tie-in exhibition showing at Proud Camden Moss,
10 Greenland Street, London NW1.
Dates: September 27th – November 18th.

Name ....

Address ....

....

....

Email ....

Tel (optional) ....

SPECIAL TRIBUTE ISSUE

NME

NEW MUSICAL EXPRESS

TOUR WARNING! **THE MUSIC**

ASS-KICKING SPACE-ROCK MAYHEM!

BE FIRST DOWN THE FRONT!
**RADIOHEAD
THE STROKES
COLDPLAY
BLACK REBEL
AUDIOSLAVE
THE WHITE STRIPES
THE CORAL
MUSE...**
...2003 GIG NEWS OVERLOAD!

CLASH LEGEND REMEMBERED

JOE STRUMMER

A true rock rebel

Pages 3, 4, 5, 20, 21, 22, 23

JACK WHITE
INTERVIEWS
ARTHUR 'LOVE' LEE

11 JANUARY 2003 £1.50 (US $4.50)
PHOTOGRAPHY: BUZZY ENTERPRISES LTD
NME.COM
MUSIC NEWS UPDATED EVERY HOUR!

02>
9 770028 636147

PLUS: EMINEM PANJABI MC THE FAINT NAS STARSAILOR

JOE STRUMMER R.I.P.

(1952 - 2002)

This section of the book was compiled at the end of January 2003, it contains tributes and guide to the last weeks of Joe's life (c/o the NME).

"The Clash were the greatest rock band. They wrote the rule book for U2. Though I was always too much of a fan to get to know him well, we were due to meet in January to finish our Nelson Mandela song with Dave Stewart. It's such a shock."

(BONO)

"Our friend and compadre is gone. God bless you, Joe."

(MICK JONES)

"We're shocked and saddened to hear of the sad loss, especially at this time of year."

(NICKY WIRE)

"At times, what he said carried uncompromising conviction and when he was done, spirits lifted, sometimes all you wanted to do was cheer."

(ALLAN JONES/UNCUT MAGAZINE)

"I met The Clash in 1976. I was a young journalist on NME and they were an unsigned band. I did their first big interview for an NME cover story in early-1977. I thought they were the greatest band I had ever seen. And half a lifetime on, in a large part of my soul, I still do."

(TONY PARSONS)

"So farewell then, Comrade Strumski. Go straight to heaven, boy. Your name's on the door. Walk right in."
(CHARLES SHAAR MURRAY)

"Joe Strummer was my greatest inspiration, my favourite singer of all time and my hero. I already miss him so much."

(TOM MORELLO)

"He was a big part of the whole punk movement."

(STEVE JONES)

"The Clash were one of those bands who were so amazing and so wonderful that people are often tempted to take them for granted. But it's worth remembering that Joe and The Clash made music that was emotional and political and challenging and experimental and exciting and wonderful."

(MOBY)

"They were unique because, here they are, breaking up at the peak of their popularity and having plenty of offers to come back, and not doing it. While other bands always come back for the money, they had belief in what they were doing, and even though they could have used it, they never really cared about the money."

(JOHNNY RAMONE)

"Joe was not just a great bloke — he was also a great musician who wasn't afraid to take a chance and write lyrics that made a difference. His death is a very sad day for the music scene. Yet again it's one of the good guys who's died young."

(GLEN MATLOCK)

"That heart of his always worked too hard. He's been making great music lately. I will really miss him."

(PETE TOWNSHEND)

"He had a very gruff singing voice but there was lots of passion. The Clash played a crucial role in punk."

(PETE SHELLEY)

"He was like an older brother or father figure to me. I listened to that first Clash album more than any other. I can't imagine what things would have been like without it."

(JOHN SQUIRE)

"I'm very, very sad at the news of Joe's death. I cannot pretend that we were that close but I am a great admirer of his songs and lyrics. The last time I saw Joe we were driving through Notting Hill at 60mph in his Hot Rod VW. I think that this says a lot about him and his spirit. My thoughts are with his family and friends."

(ELVIS COSTELLO)

"He was a clear contemporary, and we were rivals. I believed we had to get inside the pop culture. He believed you should always stay outside and hurl things at it. We had endless arguments about it. As we all got older I realised what a nice person he was."

(BOB GELDOF)

Joe Strummer Photo: Richard Young/Rex features

THE LAST WEEKS OF A ROCK LEGEND...

(NOVEMBER IITH)

Strummer starts his final UK tour with The Mescaleros. The opening night of the 'Bringing It All Back Home' tour is at the Edinburgh Liquid Rooms.

(NOVEMBER I5TH)

Strummer grabs headlines performing a show in aid of FBU at London Acton Town Hall. Clash guitarist Mick Jones joins him on stage for the first time in almost two decades. It is the closest the world will ever get to a reunion.

(NOVEMBER 22ND)

Joe Strummer plays his last ever show at Liverpool University. The set combines new material with Clash classics.

(DECEMBER 5TH)

Joe Strummer and The Mescaleros announce that they're going into the studio to work on their new album, tentatively scheduled for release in the spring.

(DECEMBER 22ND)

Strummer dies peacefully at his home in Bloomfield, Somerset, aged just 50.

Initial press reports say the cause of death is a 'suspected heart attack'.

(DECEMBER 23RD)

A simple statement is issued on Strummer's official website, which reads: "Joe Strummer died yesterday. Our condolences to Luce and the kids, family and friends". Numerous tributes flood in from all over the world from both fans and his musical peers.

(DECEMBER 24TH)

An autopsy finds Joe Strummer died of a sudden cardiac arrest, as was suspected. It emerges the singer collapsed after walking his dog. The UK press join in tribute to Strummer. The Sun call him: "The voice of a generation". The Independent both: "Influential and radical". Even the traditionally conservative Daily Mail admits he shook "The very foundations of rock music".

(DECEMBER 30TH)

Strummer is cremated at a private ceremony in West London. It is attended by his former bandmates, his close family and friends such as Fatboy Slim, Don Letts and actor Keith Allen. His coffin is adorned with a Stetson and stickers carrying the slogans 'Vinyl Rules' and 'Question Authority'.

THE CLASH AFTER JOE...

On February 13th in central London, Mick Jones, Paul Simonon and Nicky Headon attended The NME Brat Awards, to receive the award for 'Godlike Genius' on behalf of The Clash.

On March 10th in New York City, The Clash took their place in the 'Rock n' Roll Hall Of Fame'.

ABOUT THE AUTHOR:

Alan Parker was born in 1965, a great year for
selling Beatles records!
He became a music fan at the tender age of 9
after seeing Slade play live at King Georges
Hall, Blackburn. His record collection is best
described as massive, while his DVD collection
is fast catching up. As a journalist, he has
contributed to magazines including Record
Collector, Spiral Scratch, Bizarre, Ice and
The Zone. He works on re-issue campaigns for;
EMI records, Sanctuary, Strange Fruit and
Secret.

HIS PREVIOUS BOOKS INCLUDE:

SATELLITE
(Abstract Sounds Publishing)

THE GREAT TRAIN ROBBERY FILES
(Abstract Sounds Publishing)

SID'S WAY
(Omnibus Press)

TRACI LORDS: HARDCORE SUPERSTAR
(Private Publishing)

He currently lives in Maida Vale, London and
is working on books with Jonathan Richards and
Phil Strongman.

THANKS TO THE FOLLOWING:

Mick Jones, Joe Strummer, Paul Simonon & Topper
Headon (For giving me the soundtrack to my own
revolution!)

Edward Christie (For continued faith in me)

Robert Kirby (And all at PFD)

Steve Woof (For everything)

Jonathan Richards
(Without whom, it will never be forgotten)

Melissa Palmer (My 'wee me' sister)

David Parker, my brother
(For help with difficult Clash recordings)

Uncle George X (Uncrowned King of The Punks)

Don Letts (The world's hippest movie maker)

Tony Wilson (Who made Lancashire evenings
incredible!)

Everyone at King Georges Hall in Blackburn
(For giving a boy a chance!)

Mum & Dad (See eventually all dreams do come true,
thank you for your support)

Paul Burgess (Satellite kid)

Rav Singh (Take a giant step inside my mind)

Keira, Jazmin, Louise, Maz, Fi, Ellie, Ruth & Beki
(The girls, and why not!)

Simon Mattock (No One Is Innocent)

Jack 'The Hat' Kane & Andy Davis
(The tribe called Record Collector)

Graham Jones (Effectively Mr Clash!)

All the staff at Spice Of Life boozer (West
End/London)

Joe Alvarez (Just keep looking this way!)

Phil Hendriks (The Young Guitar!)

Nicky Hobbs at Sony Music
(Who really came through for me)

Jon McCaughey (The Bridge Street Mafia)

Alan Garvin (The 5th Beatle)

Pat, Wag, Mark and Uncle Tom Cobbly at Mojo
(A bible in four week shifts)

Luke Cuningham (Race You To The Grave)

Phil Strongman ("Back in the day, we...")

Mick O'Shea (The Northern Uproar!)

Everyone in the Stiff Little Fingers camp
(Especially Jake, Bruce, Steve and Ian)

Kirk Brandon & Liam Feekery
(Yes, I believe in the Westworld)

All the men in black (That's The Stranglers to
you!)

Pete Wylie (You're killing me with kindness and...)

"Punk died the day The Clash signed to CBS."
(Mark P, Sniffin' Glue)